The Lesbian Idol

The Lesbian Idol

Martina, kd and the Consumption of Lesbian Masculinity

Louise Allen

CASSELL

London and Washington

For a catalogue of related titles in our
Sexual Politics/Global Issues list please write to us
at the address below.

Cassell
Wellington House
125 Strand
London WC2R 0BB

PO Box 605
Herndon, VA 20172

First published 1997

British Library Cataloguing in Publication Data

A catalogue record for this book is available from the British Library.

ISBN   0–304–33818–4 (hardback)

0–304–33819–2 (paperback)

Designed and typeset by Ben Cracknell Studios

Printed and bound in Great Britain by Biddles Ltd, Guildford and King's Lynn

Contents

Acknowledgements

I am extremely grateful to all the lesbian fans of kd and Martina who wrote to me about their idols – by sharing their personal experiences they provided valuable material for this study. I would particularly like to thank Sarah Franklin and Jackie Stacey for reading numerous drafts of this book and providing highly appreciated intellectual and academic insight and guidance, as well as for their continuing encouragement. Also for reading and commenting on earlier drafts of this book, I am grateful to Richard Dyer, Celia Lury, Lynne Pearce, Margrit Shildrick and Beverley Skeggs. I am grateful to Lancaster University for funding this research, and to Roz Hopkins, my editor at Cassell. I also wish to thank my mum, Jean, for her support, and Sarah-Line Letellier for her patience, and for helping with the later stages of the book.

This book is dedicated to
Sarah-Line Letellier

1

Lesbian Culture is Everywhere

Since the mid-1980s we have seen an unprecedented increase in the representation of lesbian identity in the Anglo-American mainstream media; this popularization of lesbianism has occurred across diverse forms of visual media and across various cultural sites. There has been repeated 'coverage' of lesbian identity in film, television drama and documentary, soap opera, popular fashion, and also in music and lifestyle magazines. This recent fascination with lesbianism exemplifies how lesbian sexuality has become something of a *commodity* within western consumer culture. My analysis of lesbian identity in the 1990s in this book will be informed by a critique of this phenomenon popularly known as 'lesbian chic'.[1] Against this analysis, and the recent 'spectaclization' of the lesbian, I will posit a study of a concurrent, but in many ways different, phenomenon – lesbian stardom and fandom. In this exploration of the lesbian star/fan relationship I will concentrate on the consumption of specific lesbian idols by their lesbian fans. I will also examine the crucial ways in which process of recognition, identification and desire in the lesbian star/fan relationship set this apart from the explosion of lesbian chic in the mainstream media.

Using kd lang and Martina Navratilova as examples of lesbian idols, I will examine in a specifically British context how lesbian identity signifies and is consumed in different ways and in different specific cultural contexts. These stars at once exemplify, but also are separable from, an increasing commodification of lesbian sexuality in the media. Here, I analyse the representation and consumption of lesbian idols in relation to the phenomenon of lesbian idols. Thus I will explore how both photographic representations of kd and Martina, and the accounts of the consumption of these lesbian stars by their lesbian fans, contribute to the construction of lesbian identity in relation to gender, race and ethnicity. I will also conduct my own analysis of the images and knowledges through which Martina and kd and lesbian chic are discursively reproduced in specific social and cultural spaces.

It is, therefore, important to stress why the representation of kd and Martina is not necessarily representative of the broader popularization of lesbianism in the media. Whilst lesbian chic draws on conventional images of femininity, the representation of Martina and kd reproduces traditional ideas and signifiers of masculinity. The media popularization of lesbianism through codes of femininity informs a popular construction of lesbian chic which has decorated the pages of both straight and lesbian-oriented publications;[2] in contrast, kd and Martina are popular as lesbian idols *precisely because* of the way they are represented via conventional codes of masculinity. I will hence explore the question of whether this representation of lesbianism which draws on codes of masculinity is more troubling to, and disruptive of, heterosexual gender norms than representations of lesbian chic, and, further, whether the lesbian star/fan relationship may undermine dominant heterosexual marketing and consumption strategies.

Martina has been in the public eye in Britain as a world-class tennis champion since her first victory at Wimbledon in 1978. Because of her defection from Czechoslovakia to the USA, and her subsequent record-breaking nine victories in the women's singles championships at Wimbledon, she received much media attention throughout her career. Her lesbian affairs also kept her in the public eye. After a liaison with novelist Rita-Mae Brown in 1979, she had a relationship with fellow sportswoman Nancy Lieberman in 1981. In 1984 she left Lieberman to set up home with Judy Nelson, until they 'divorced' in 1991 – the same year she finally came out as a lesbian. As Martina's singles career ended (she last competed in the singles championships in 1994), so her visibility in lesbian and gay activism increased. In 1993 she spoke to a crowd of 500,000 at the Lesbian and Gay March on Washington, receiving a standing ovation even before she reached the platform.

Martina's significance as a tennis champion is equalled by her importance as a lesbian idol and role model for thousands of lesbians throughout the world. Her televised performances at Wimbledon every year since 1978 must remain the most sustained media coverage of a single lesbian in history, and her many lesbian fans have also had repeated opportunities to see her 'live' at matches throughout the world tennis circuit. For these reasons I have chosen to examine her status as a lesbian idol.

kd lang also struggled to international stardom in her chosen career of music. She started out as an 'alternative' performer/singer in rural Canada, writing her first song at the age of thirteen and singing it to her classmates at school. In the early 1980s, whilst still living in Canada, she developed an interest in country music, and formed the band The Reclines, named after her singing idol Patsy Cline, on whom she modelled herself. Eventually she went solo, and her debut album *A Truly Western Experience* (1984) marked her successful entrance into the country music business. She brought out a series of albums in country and western style, *Angel with a Lariat* (1987), *Shadowland* (1988) and *Absolute Torch and Twang* (1989), later developing her own music style which was less influenced by the country music tradition and hailed by some as more 'mainstream'.[3] This move resulted in the album *Ingénue* (1992), which firmly established her as an internationally successful musician.

Ingénue was more successful than previous albums in terms of 'mass' or 'popular' appeal, and it attracted both a heterosexual audience, and a more specific audience of lesbian fans. Although a smaller lesbian audience had been attracted by her dress style and short hair in her earlier career in country music, the release of *Ingénue* signalled a frenzied surge of lesbian popular music fandom, which was further encouraged when kd came out to the American magazine *The Advocate* in 1992. In August 1993 kd's photo-shoot with Cindy Crawford for *Vanity Fair* established her even more firmly within the 'lesbian idol' league. Other albums have followed: *Even Cowgirls Get the Blues* (1993) was the soundtrack for the Gus Van Sant movie of the same name, and 1995 saw the release of *All You Can Eat*. She has repeatedly featured in many music and lifestyle magazines, and on a variety of music and entertainment shows in Britain. When she tours the country her shows are sold out to a vast majority of lesbian fans.

The importance of kd and Martina as role models and idols for lesbian consumption convinced me to take the lesbian star/fan relationship as the starting point for my research. It would allow me to analyse both the most contemporary issues surrounding lesbianism, and the most contemporary visual images of lesbians being produced in the media. The rapidly changing visual culture, characteristic of the late twentieth century, coupled with an academic field of enquiry – loosely termed poststructuralism[4] or postmodernism[5] – that emphasizes shifting identity positions, made it important for me to analyse to what extent privileging systems of difference were either strengthened or challenged in such a context. *The Lesbian Idol* thus explores the relationship between meaning, image and identity across a field that I want to term 'lesbian culture'; consequently, then, this book is also, in one sense, an attempt to map out that field.

What is Lesbian Culture?

Since I first started writing about lesbianism in 1989 I have been concerned with developing an approach to lesbian culture which emphasizes the lived experience of lesbians as well as the textual representation of that culture – an approach that would make sense of how lesbians live their lives situated within increasingly frenetic discourses of identity politics, lifestyle, dress codes, lesbian chic, butch and femme, parody, performance, masquerade and so on; discourses which have featured prominently in recent articles about lesbian culture.[6] It therefore became clear that I needed to adopt a multi-textual approach to the study of lesbian culture; in other words, an approach which would enable me to critique general pertinent themes through theoretical discourses, my own textual analysis of visual images and a kind of 'ethnographic'[7] study of lesbian fans' accounts of lesbian stars. Using this method I believed that I could track aspects of lesbian culture that posed a potential threat to heterosexual domination (such as lesbian stardom/fandom) through various realms of theoretical knowledge, such as queer theory, psychoanalysis, feminist theory, cultural theory and lesbian theory, and also via my own interpretation of the contemporary visual culture that pertains to lesbians and an analysis of the accounts of lesbian subjects.

Considering that my research focuses on lesbian stars and fans, I work with certain tensions regarding the use of the category 'lesbian'. On the one hand, the term 'lesbian' does have purchase as an identity category, because people live their lives in relation to that category. On the other hand, the term 'lesbian' denotes a multi-valence of meanings about what a lesbian 'is'. I therefore address *how* lesbian identifications and cultures are engaged in a dialogue with heterosexual knowledge systems whereby meanings and values are inscribed across various circuits of representation. I suggest throughout this book that meanings are derived in a relationship between text and contextualized viewing experiences and that differences with regards to meanings reproduce cultural differences and specificities; hence it becomes possible to talk of a 'lesbian gaze'.

I wanted to introduce the study of lesbian culture by highlighting the themes I felt should frame any such analysis. However, I am not claiming that this book provides a blueprint for a definitive approach; rather that the development of multi-textual studies in this area highlights the interconnected, contradictory and often confusing ways of living and identifying that seem to have characterized lesbian culture in the 1990s so far. Before embarking on such a project, it is important to address just what we mean by 'lesbian culture'. In *Lesbian Choices*, Claudia Card asks this very question:

> I hear the question 'What is lesbian culture?' with the emphasis on lesbian. And I hear 'Culture' not necessarily as *a* culture, or cultures, but as lesbian developments within many cultures that would not usually be aptly described themselves as lesbian. 'Culture' has many meanings. It is, for example, ambiguous between 'the behaviors and beliefs characteristic of a particular social, ethnic, or age *group*,' on the one hand and, on another, 'the sum total ways of living built up by a group of human beings and *transmitted from one generation to another*.' There has been little opportunity for lesbian culture in the second sense. Even with respect to the first sense, lesbians are not *a* social group but many social groups or, as I will suggest, a 'family' of social groups. By studying lesbian culture as the behaviors and beliefs characteristic of many groups of lesbians, preserving and appreciating what we find and passing it on, we may contribute to the development of lesbian culture in the second sense.[8]

Card's definition of lesbian culture is important because she shows how difficult it is to talk of lesbian culture at all. As she notes, lesbians are diverse and individuated, and the striking lack of lesbian cultural 'groups' is perhaps explained by the fact that lesbianism is non-genealogical, unlike race, ethnicity and even, to some extent, religion. Another reason why lesbian culture is difficult to establish is that throughout history what we may term lesbian practice has centred around leisure and political activities. Thus, the traditional signifiers of culture on which these activities often rest (for example, the genealogical relationships that have informed the black civil rights movement) are missing. Also to define the lesbian sex act as a signifier of culture is problematic, as women who may practise sex with women, whilst enjoying a privileged heterosexual lifestyle, remain indistinguishable from lesbians.[9]

Nevertheless, despite these many problems, I think that it is important to have an understanding of lesbian culture. To discuss variable and interconnecting sets of practices as culture may mean thinking about culture in a way that differs from the traditional anthropological or even more recent sociological definitions. This would involve consideration of how we understand lesbianism, lesbian identity and lesbian identifications from the viewpoint of living and working as lesbians in different social contexts and in relation to various forms of domination.

Such an analysis of lesbian culture must be set within the context of a wider western culture, and at a particular historical conjuncture. Regarding the issue of historic specificity, my particular study requires a different kind of approach than would have been appropriate ten years ago. The rapid increase in the representation of lesbianism in the media since the mid-1980s highlights the need to continually re-evaluate how we think about lesbian culture.

Mariana Valverde, writing in 1985, discusses lesbianism in relation to history, invisibility, eroticism, pornography, pleasure and ethics and feminist politics. In a short subsection on 'lesbian culture' she notes that any discussion of the issue involves recourse to the lesbian novel, a clear indication of how few images of lesbianism were available throughout the popular visual media in the mid-1980s. Significantly, she uses the term 'lesbian culture' to describe cultural production about and by lesbians:

> There are a couple of themes that emerge from an examination of the lesbian culture that has developed over the past ten or fifteen years. I am talking primarily about lesbian literature, and to a lesser extent music, since we have not yet been able to make many films or produce much visual art. This is partly due to financial factors and sale and distribution problems. But it is also due to certain inherent problems in portraying women's bodies erotically without having those depictions interpreted as pornographic. In any case, in women's, gay, and progressive bookstores one can find quite a number of literary works that allow us to make some tentative comments about trends and recurring ideals.[10]

The focus Valverde places on the financial obstacles to the development of a lesbian culture, and her concern about pornographic visual representations of lesbians is significant in terms of the ways in which we should be interrogating the sudden increase in lesbian representation. From the emphasis Valverde places on the dearth of lesbian visual culture in her analysis, one would assume that at least fifty, and not ten, years had passed between her analysis and my own.

As well as the historical variants that must inform any analysis of lesbian culture, we also need to recognize that lesbian culture is inherently fractured, diverse and changeable, but with common threads or strands of knowledge, belief systems and sets of practices that distinguish or characterize 'lesbians', as Card has astutely suggested. We also need to understand how such diverse yet interrelated threads determine particular ways of living as lesbians, and how this might – particularly in view of the rise of lesbian parenting – lead to the transmission of these ways of living 'from one generation to another'.[11]

Thus we also need an analysis of lesbian culture which critically engages with the cultural production associated with this culture – production generated both *by* lesbians (for example, magazines, idols, art, photography, theory, fiction, fashion) and by dominant culture *about* lesbians (tabloid news stories, stereotypical imagery); in addition, it must encompass the regimes of knowledge that pervade and inform lesbian ways of living (for example, queer, lesbian chic, butch/femme, the essentialism/constructionism debate, passing, genetics, bisexuality, homophobia, as well as sexism, racism, classism and anti-Semitism). In other words, we should not regard 'lesbian culture' as a homogenous group or cluster of lesbians going about their everyday lives, but, rather, in a way that suggests an interconnected realm of practices, thoughts, values, ideas, knowledges, experiences and differences, through and across which both alliances and power struggles persist. Such a realm may consist of debates in lesbian theory, political action by lesbians, the production of visual culture by lesbians and critiques of the reception of cultural items produced by the dominant culture 'in the name of lesbianism'. However, such a realm may also exist in the minds of lesbians, in the recollection of lesbian pasts or in beliefs about how the world should be.

Researching Lesbian Culture

My preference for a multi-textual approach and my underlying understanding of how to define lesbian culture, in one sense, co-constituted each other during the writing of this book. My primary interest has been in theoretical issues concerning identity, and I was influenced by the debates between lesbian theorists in the late 1980s. I particularly drew inspiration from the issues discussed in Diana Fuss's *Essentially Speaking*[12] and Judith Butler's *Gender Trouble*.[13] Whilst keen to engage with non-theoretical

7

material – images and the accounts of lesbian consumers – I also wanted to retain a theoretical focus. This was primarily because I felt concerned about the way that notions of shifting identities, performance, parody, butch/femme and drag structured a new mode of lesbian theory which drew heavily on poststructuralist ideas of identity and yet also followed Butler's and Fuss's more feminist-oriented analyses.[14] To me, this new lesbian theory meant that lesbian identity and culture were becoming abstracted almost beyond recognition, and that more and more lesbian theorists were less and less willing to engage with lesbian audiences.

In my exploration of photographic images I have attempted in this book to illustrate the ways in which dominant discourses are reproduced in visual terms, but also, importantly, how such discourses may be challenged through lesbian readership practices. However, I was faced with the problem of how to link my analysis of photographic images, queer theory, fetishism and lesbian theory to lesbian cultural practice, as I wanted to ascertain how lesbians responded to, and lived in relation to, particular kinds of visual imagery, knowledges and discourses around lesbianism.

I realized that this would require some kind of analysis which would come under a broad heading of 'ethnography'. So, I decided to contact lesbians to find out about how they lived, and their views and opinions. Rather than an open-ended analysis of lesbians, I conducted a study of one aspect of lesbian life. Therefore, I narrowed the field of enquiry down to two famous and publicly out lesbian idols and their fans. I decided to advertise for lesbian fans to write to me about their idols. In this sense I believed that my research would depart from the heavily sociological academic studies that employ qualitative research methodologies, and would instead contribute to an ever-increasing body of feminist research and research into stars, fans and audiences of popular culture in general.

Work on the relationship between stars and their audiences is rare; although much has been written on stardom itself, and on particular stars, only a handful of recent studies have engaged with the star/fan relationship using audience research. Jackie Stacey's recent contribution to this field, *Star Gazing*,[15] has greatly influenced my project. In this book she analyses female consumers of 1940s and 1950s Hollywood film stars, and their recollections of visiting cinemas and idolizing their stars. Jacqueline Bobo[16] explores how black women engage with cultural texts such as novels and films; using interviews and textual readings she provides an important study of black women as consumers. In Richard Dyer's *Heavenly Bodies*,[17] the author relates iconic male and female film stars to gay culture and identifications in a cultural analysis that combines his own readings of films with knowledges and experiences particular to the gay subculture.

Few recent articles or books about lesbians have engaged with ethnographic material. Kath Weston's ethnographic study of lesbian and gay kinship includes interviews with many gays and lesbians and identifies the major themes which structure contemporary lesbian and gay life, such as relationships with straight families, coming-out narratives, love and lesbian motherhood.[18] Elizabeth Lapovsky Kennedy and Madeline D. Davis have conducted perhaps the most comprehensive analysis into lesbian culture. Their book, *Boots of Leather, Slippers of Gold* follows a lesbian community in Buffalo, New York, from the mid-1930s to the early 1960s, and uses histories collected from 45 women. They describe their work thus:

> *Boots of Leather, Slippers of Gold* is the first book-length study of a mid-century bar community. Focusing on Buffalo, New York, the book aims to explore how the culture of resistance that developed in working-class lesbian bars and house parties contributed to shaping twentieth-century gay and lesbian consciousness and politics. Our approach is that of ethno-history: a combination of the methodology of ethnography – the intensive study of the culture and identity of a single community – with history – the analysis of the forces that shaped how that community changed over time, using as our primary sources oral histories of Buffalo lesbians.[19]

Two examples of research into lesbian media audiences are, first, an article entitled 'Hollywood Transformed: Interviews with Lesbian Viewers', in which Claire Whitaker interviews lesbians about their favourite cinematic experiences,[20] and secondly, Julia Hallam and Margaret Marshment's analysis of audiences of the television drama *Oranges Are Not the Only Fruit*.[21] There have been only a handful of articles about the lesbian stars kd and Martina;[22] none of which include ethnographic material. Thus I felt there was a need to combine an 'ethnographic study' of lesbian culture with the star/fan relationship specific to the consumption of these lesbian idols, particularly as the wealth of information that could be collected from fans[23] would, I hoped, also involve the generation of a significant body of empirical data.

In the period between August 1993 and April 1994 I published a letter in the London-based gay and lesbian publications the *Pink Paper* and

Rouge, the lesbian-produced newsletter *Lesbian London*, the Scottish publications *Harpies and Quines* and *Gay Scotland*, the North of England-based arts magazine *Northern Star* and the kd fanzine *Highway Twelve*. I also distributed requests for correspondence amongst people I had made contact with whilst conducting the research, and several respondents offered to distribute requests amongst friends and in gay and lesbian bars in their home towns. The letter I published read as follows:

> Are you a lesbian? Do you like kd lang or Martina Navratilova? Or do you hate them? If you have strong feelings either way I would like to hear from you. I am a lesbian researcher working in this area.
>
> If you would like to help me, please submit a letter as long as possible (anonymously if you like) about either or both of these stars. Please say what you like/don't like about them and why, how they have influenced you, if and where you have seen them, what memorabilia you have collected, what you would say if you met them, etc.

I asked respondents to send me a long letter so that I had as much data to work with as possible, and I introduced the possibilty of anonymity so that more responses might be forthcoming. I wanted respondents to say why they either *liked or disliked* kd or Martina because I thought that if they had strong feelings either way this would provide important, and interesting, material to study. The requests for details of memorabilia they had collected, and what they would say if they met their idol, was designed to give respondents the opportunity to relate more personal accounts of experiences, identifications and desires. I hoped that making my own lesbianism explicit would encourage more people to reply. I also wanted only to address the respondents as 'lesbians' in my research, in order to isolate lesbianism from other areas of identification – I did not want my analysis to be *exclusive* but, rather, *specific*.

The response confirmed that I had been correct to keep my original letter very simple, as I received nearly fifty letters between October 1993 and August 1994. Many contained pages of narrative detail that recounted deep emotions, desires, loyalty and personal experiences that astounded me in their intensity. As the letters were so confessional and personal, I decided to change the names of *all* respondents to ensure anonymity, regardless of whether they had requested it or not. Significantly, most respondents told me their age and, often, chronologically charted their development both as kd or Martina fans and as lesbians (this was probably because in lesbian narratives, age can be an important indicator as to how long someone has been 'out'). In terms of religion, some letters told of strict Catholic upbringings which had significantly hindered coming out processes.

I believe that lesbian culture should also be discussed in terms of racial discourse, and am aware that I may well be accused of being 'silent' on the issue of race myself – why didn't I say I was a white lesbian researcher, or that I wanted to hear from only white lesbians? Importantly, though, one of my research questions concerned the issue of how to examine white privilege in lesbian culture; to this end I decided not to foreground the issue of race and see what the letters revealed. Far from remaining silent on the issue of race, the replies helped me to identify ways in which racial or ethnic discourses and racist, ethnic and nationalist stereotypes were deployed in order to describe kd or Martina.

Importantly, I work with the idea that racial and class signifiers are always already embedded in the inscription of gender meanings at the level of representation, and that privileges of whiteness and class pervade representations of lesbianism. Here I focus on a kind of gender privilege that pervades the representation of lesbianism in the mainstream media, whereby the feminine lesbian has become the signifier of lesbian chic, and the masculine lesbian has become the signifier of all that is wrong with lesbianism in the 1990s. This gender privilege is further compounded by the way that masculine lesbians seem to receive the full force of a dominating homophobic gaze. These differing representations of masculine and feminine lesbians in the mainstream media is a central issue in this study, and through this understanding of gender privilege I have been able to interrogate how whiteness is secured as an ideal racial identity in this context.

Writing Lesbian Culture

My aim is to contrast two modes of the representation of lesbianism: that of lesbian chic in mainstream media contexts, and that of lesbian idols in both mainstream and lesbian-oriented media. Using a multi-textual approach, I trace theoretical trends of queer and psychoanalysis, conduct readings of photographic imagery and analyse the accounts of lesbian fans. This approach enables me to argue that lesbian chic is a reactionary strategy on the part of the dominant media that undermines what is at stake for those who wish to identify as lesbians whilst living, and trying to develop cultures, within a deeply homophobic and patriarchal British society.

Bearing in mind the approach to lesbian culture I have outlined in this chapter, Chapter Two will pay critical attention to pervasive theoretical perspectives which, relate to and inform lesbian culture and have affected the development of this culture in recent years – most notably the growth of what I term *lesbian theory*. Lesbian academia has, to a large extent, been dominated by those who favour theories put forward by Judith Butler in *Gender Trouble*.[24] However, I shall also examine the theories Teresa de Lauretis puts forward in her recent book *The Practice of Love*,[25] and analyse the contribution of Elisabeth Grosz[26] to this emerging field of lesbian theory.

Importantly, I juxtapose my analysis of this development of a specifically lesbian theory against the simultaneous rise of queer theory. Examining the queer theories of Jonathan Dollimore[27] and Eve Sedgwick,[28] I shall argue that their analyses of the centrality of homosexuality in western culture are, ironically, so deeply homophobic that they cannot include lesbians. In my view the lack of distinction between lesbian and queer theories has hampered a proper understanding and discussion of the drastic changes in lesbian culture that have occurred over the past ten years. Importantly, queer theories which exclude lesbianism have *oppressed* lesbian-specific theories (it has been difficult for specifically lesbian theories to develop), but also have *radically informed* such theories (when lesbian theories do develop, central tenets of queer theory often structure them). This is a significant problem, because queer theory, in one sense, actively pre-empts a theoretical approach to lesbianism. This divisive move in the academy thus suppresses an examination of the various means by which lesbians are oppressed, not only through heterosexuality but also through the gay theoretical practice of Dollimore and the 'gay-affirmative' theoretical practice of Sedgwick.

In this book, then, I put forward a radical critique of the use of queer theory in an analysis of lesbian culture, and also develop my own mode of theorizing about lesbian culture which draws on a mixture of cultural, feminist and lesbian theory. Chapter Three, in particular, contains textual analyses of various visual media representations of lesbian stars and lesbian chic; in my exploration of these images I rely on a notion of the importance of the production of meaning via lesbian-specific consumption practices. My own readings of these images follow a model made popular by feminist cultural studies in the late 1970s and the 1980s.[29] This model intersperses an analysis of the modes and conditions of the production of the images with an examination of the dominant meanings and discourses which are produced in relation to specific images.

In Chapter Four, in a move to extend my criticism of queer theory and the problematic emergence of lesbian chic, I examine the notion of lesbian fetishism that has become so popular in lesbian theory over the past decade. Whilst most of psychoanalytic theory has been dismissed by lesbian theorists on the grounds of sexism and homophobia, it seems, however, that fetishism remains central to many understandings of what it means to be a lesbian. In this chapter I examine Freud's theory of fetishism and some of the rereadings of Freud that have taken place within lesbian theory. These appropriations of Freud's notion of fetishism, perhaps best exemplified by de Lauretis's analysis in *The Practice of Love*, argue that fetishism, along with other Freudian concepts such as the 'masculinity complex' and the 'castration complex', should be re-examined by lesbians as a radical realm where heterosexual oppression may be overturned.

Included in this chapter are images of kd and Martina that draw on the notion of fetishism; however, I suggest that their lesbian fans *do not* consume these images *fetishistically*. On the contrary, I suggest that lesbian fans find pleasure in looking at, and articulate desire in relation to, such images *in spite of* that fetishism through which they become immediately meaningful. The negotiation of fetishism by lesbians is thus central to my analysis of the lesbian star/fan relationship, because I argue that lesbian theorists should permanently disengage from psychoanalytic theory, unless it is to talk about psychoanalysis as the object of study rather than a vehicle within which to theorize.

In Chapter Five I analyse in detail the letters sent to me by lesbian fans of Martina and kd, examining the construction of lesbian identities through the proliferation of lesbian experiences, desires and fantasies in this lesbian star/fan context, and also questioning whether this relationship may disrupt those conventional notions of sexual and gender difference which are secured in the heterosexual star/fan context. I also explore how understandings of ethnicity may be reproduced through such consumption practices and discuss the letters as lesbian romantic texts. I wanted to find a way to talk about lesbian desire that neither described lesbian practices as fetishistic nor drew on psychoanalytic theory, as much recent lesbian theory has done.[30] Therefore, I decided to use the notion of romance (also recently made popular by lesbian theorists[31]) to examine how a traditional heterosexual romantic narrative is disrupted by a lesbian gaze, through which a masculine lesbian is desired.

Lesbian Culture: It's All Academic Now

Aside from a recent increase in the representation of lesbians in the media, there has also been a rise in the amount of academic work published about lesbian culture over the past ten years, and it is important to comment on this phenomenon before I proceed with my theoretical arguments. Since the 1980s there has been a shift in the subject matter of academic books on lesbianism. In 1988 Virago published *Out the Other Side: Contemporary Lesbian Writing*.[32] Among the subjects covered in this collection are the issue of lesbianism in relation to feminism, which arose out of the great s/m debate of late 1980s; the issue of diversity and coalition within and between lesbians and feminists; difference; experiences of lesbian mothering; the menopause; the issue of feminism in relation to AIDS; racism, and a few autobiographical pieces. No article directly discussed lesbianism in relation to the popular media.

Sex and Love: New Thoughts on Old Contradictions was first published in 1983.[33] This book brings lesbianism and feminism together and contains essays on feminism, psychoanalysis and the analysis of lesbianism in the 1970s.[34] Although less lesbian-specific, *Desire: The Politics of Sexuality*[35] and *Pleasure and Danger: Exploring Female Sexuality*[36] are, however, useful resources for lesbian academics and non-academics alike. *Desire* covers such topics as feminism and pornography, class and female sexuality, and abortion, along with lesbian sex roles and gay male identity. *Pleasure and Danger* adopts a similar angle and includes essays on the politically correct and feminist sexual politics.

However, in more recent academic editions about lesbianism, the popular media has emerged as a central focus. Four edited collections of lesbian theory in particular exemplify this shift. *Outwrite: Lesbianism and Popular Culture*[37] includes articles on lesbian cinema, lesbian popular music, the lesbian thriller novel and the media representation of lesbian sex. *Daring to Dissent: Lesbian Culture from Margin to Mainstream*[38] contains writing about lesbian queer cinema, specific films such as *The Hunger*, the lesbian mystery novel, lesbians and television, and lesbians and the radio. Published in 1994, *The Good, the Bad and the Gorgeous: Popular Culture's Romance with Lesbianism*[39] examines issues such as the relationship between Madonna and lesbian culture, lesbians and country music, the career and stardom of Martina Navratilova, Jodie Foster as a lesbian cult figure, the documentary series *Out*, and specific films and television programmes such as *Basic Instinct, Portrait of a Marriage, Oranges Are Not the Only Fruit* and *LA Law*. A 1995 collection, *Immortal, Invisible: Lesbians and the Moving Image*,[40] concentrates on the representation of lesbians in film and television and includes writing on the films *Salmonberries* and *Desert Hearts*, as well as other articles on related issues such as camp and fashion.

There is a striking difference in content between these titles and the publications of the late 1980s I have mentioned. The emphasis has changed from political aspects of lesbianism, with a specific focus on feminist politics, to notions of lesbian culture and identity that focus on wider, and particularly visual, popular culture. Of course, these edited collections provide an example of just one arena where the discussion of lesbian culture has changed over the past few years. A shift in focus can also be detected in refereed journals. Issues of lifestyle, fashion, music and idolization have even generated particular lesbian-produced magazines in Britain such as *Diva*, which in a subheading refers to itself as 'the lesbian lifestyle magazine'.

Within this rapidly emerging 'canon' of lesbian theory, some lesbian and gay edited collections reference a 'queer' identity. For example, *Sisters, Sexperts, Queers: Beyond the Lesbian Nation*[41] and *Out in Culture: Gay, Lesbian and Queer Essays on Popular Culture*.[42] In the next chapter I will discuss the issue of queer identity and theory in detail; however, it is important to note here that queer identity is being placed firmly within discourses of lesbianism through academic channels. All I will say here is that this emphasis on queer presents us with a significant problem: in the *Out in Culture* collection, for instance, if the gays and lesbians are identified in the title, who exactly is 'queer'? Thus, this shift in academia not only (and quite rightly) places importance on specific instances of visual and literary culture within which lesbians are represented, but has also quite deliberately (and problematically) adopted 'queerness' as part of lesbian culture. In the next chapter I will suggest that the homophobia structuring a particular mode of 'queer theory' in academia radically underscores the homophobia characteristic of the commodification of lesbian chic in the media, and that, indeed, the popularization of queer in the academy has similarities with this commodification of lesbian chic

– queer theory is distinctly saleable in the academic arena, as is lesbian chic in the popular media.

Notes

1. For an excellent critical analysis of lesbian chic see Laura Cottingham, *Lesbians Are So Chic ... that We're Not Really Lesbians at All* (London and New York: Cassell, 1996); and for further books and articles which discuss this 'lesbian chic' phenomenon also see Danae Clark, 'Commodity Lesbianism', *Camera Obscura*, Vol. 25–6, 1991, pp. 180–201; Arlene Stein, 'All Dressed Up, But no Place to Go? Style Wars and the New Lesbianism' in Joan Nestle (ed.), *The Persistent Desire: A Butch-Femme Reader* (Boston: Alyson, 1992), pp. 431–9, and 'The Year of the Lustful Lesbian' in Arlene Stein (ed.), *Sisters, Sexperts, Queers: Beyond the Lesbian Nation* (New York: Plume, 1993), pp. 13–34; Elizabeth Wilson, 'Deviant Dress', *Feminist Review* 35, Summer 1990, pp. 67–74. For articles by apologists of lesbian chic see Charlotte Cripps and Laura Tennant, 'Sappho So Good', *Harpers and Queen*, June 1994, pp. 122–7; Sian Pattenden, 'Hello Girls! The New Lesbian Cool: Everybody Else Is Doing It ... Why Can't WE?', *Select*, June 1994, pp. 60–8.

2. In 'Now a Word from Our Sponsor: The Emergence of a Gay Management Class and Its Impact on the Print Media', a paper given at the University of California at San Diego, 17 January 1994, pp. 1–15, Sarah Schulman argues that, recently, images in both the mainstream and the lesbian and gay media have become indistinguishable.

3. See Rosa Ainley and Sarah Cooper, 'Who's Conning Who?', *Trouble and Strife*, No. 23, Spring 1992, pp. 11–15.

4. For a discussion of poststructuralism see Rosalind Coward and John Ellis, *Language and Materialism: Developments in Semiology and the Theory of the Subject* (London and New York: Routledge, 1993); Julian Henriques, Couze Venn, Wendy Holloway and Valerie Walkerdine (eds), *Changing the Subject: Psychology, Social Regulation and Subjectivity* (London: Methuen, 1984); Chris Weedon, *Feminist Practice and Poststructuralist Theory* (Oxford: Basil Blackwell, 1987); and for an introduction to both poststructuralism and postmodernism see Madan Sarup, *An Introductory Guide to Poststructuralism and Postmodernism* (Hemel Hempstead: Harvester Wheatsheaf, 1988).

5. For a discussion of postmodernism see Jean Baudrillard, *For a Critique of the Political Economy of the Sign* (St Louis: Telos Press, 1981) and *Simulations* (New York: Semiotext(e), 1983); Mike Featherstone, *Consumer Culture and Postmodernism* (London: Sage, 1993); Linda Nicholson (ed.), *Feminism/Postmodernism* (London and New York: Routledge 1990); Scott Lash (ed.), *Post-structuralist and Post-modernist Sociology* (Aldershot: Edward Elgar, 1991). For a discussion of lesbian postmodernism see Laura Doan (ed.), *The Lesbian Postmodern* (New York: Columbia University Press, 1994).

6. See, for example, Sue Ellen Case, 'Toward a Butch-Femme Aesthetic' in Linda Hart (ed.), *Making a Spectacle: Feminist Essays on Contemporary Women's Theatre* (Michigan: University of Michigan Press, 1989), pp. 282–99; Stein, 'All Dressed Up'; Lisa Kahaleole Chang Hall 'Bitches in Solitude: Identity Politics and Lesbian Community' in Stein (ed.), *Sisters, Sexperts, Queers*, pp. 218–29.

7. Although this study is not characteristic of traditional sociological or anthropological ethnography, it is broadly ethnographic, in that it uses material gathered from an identified culture in order to examine that culture.

8. Claudia Card, *Lesbian Choices* (New York: Columbia University Press, 1995), pp. 12–13.

9. In 'Is There a Lesbian Culture?' in Jeffner Allen (ed.), *Lesbian Philosophies and Cultures* (New York: State University of New York, 1990), pp. 63–84, Ann Ferguson argues that an understanding of lesbian culture should be based on politics.

10. Mariana Valverde, *Sex, Power and Pleasure* (Toronto: The Women's Press, 1985), p. 100.

11. Card, *Lesbian Choices*, p. 12.

12. Diana Fuss, *Essentially Speaking: Feminism, Nature and Difference* (London and New York: Routledge, 1989).

13. Judith Butler, *Gender Trouble: Feminism and the Subversion of Identity* (London and New York, Routledge, 1990).

14. See Case, 'A Butch-Femme Aesthetic', and also Lisa M. Walker, 'How to Recognise a Lesbian: The Cultural Politics of Looking Like What You Are', *Signs*, Vol. 18 No. 4, Summer 1993, pp. 866–90.

15. Jackie Stacey, *Star Gazing* (London: Routledge, 1994).

16. Jacqueline Bobo, *Black Women as Cultural Readers* (New York and Chichester, West Sussex: Columbia University Press, 1995).

17. Richard Dyer, *Heavenly Bodies: Film Stars and Society* (London: BFI/Macmillan, 1992).

18. Kath Weston, *Families We Choose: Lesbians, Gays, Kinship* (New York: Columbia University Press, 1991).

19. Elizabeth Lapovsky Kennedy and Madeline D. Davis, *Boots of Leather, Slippers of Gold: The History of a Lesbian Community* (London and New York: Routledge, 1993), p. 2.

20. Claire Whitaker, 'Hollywood Transformed: Interviews with Lesbian Viewers' in Peter Steven (ed.), *Jump Cut: Hollywood, Politics and Counter-Cinema* (Toronto: Between The Lines, 1985), pp. 106–18.

21. Julia Hallam and Margaret Marshment, 'Framing Experience: Case Studies in the Reception of *Oranges Are Not the Only Fruit*', *Screen*, Vol. 36 No. 1, Spring 1995, pp. 1–15.

22. See Diane Hamer, 'Netting the Press: Playing with Martina' in Belinda Budge and Diane Hamer (eds), *The Good, the Bad and the Gorgeous: Popular Culture's Romance with Lesbianism* (London and San Francisco: Pandora, 1994), pp. 57–77; Gillian Rodgerson, 'Nothing to Hide', *Gay Times*, July 1993, pp. 57–9; Ainley and Cooper, 'Who's Conning Who?'.

23. See Fred Vermorel and Judy Vermorel, 'A Glimpse at the Fan Factory' in Lisa A. Lewis (ed.), *The Adoring Audience: Fan Culture and Popular Media* (London and New York: Routledge, 1992), pp. 191–207.

24. David Bell, Jon Binnie, Julian Cream and Gill Valentine rely heavily on Judith Butler's theories in 'All Hyped Up and No Place to Go', *Gender,*

Place and Culture: A Journal of
Feminist Geography, Vol. 1 No. 1,
1994, pp. 31–47.

25. Teresa de Lauretis, The Practice of
Love: Lesbian Sexuality and Perverse
Desire (Bloomington and
Indianapolis: Indiana University
Press, 1994).

26. Elizabeth Grosz, 'Lesbian
Fetishism?', Differences, Vol. 3 No.
2, Summer 1991, pp. 39–54;
'Refiguring Lesbian Desire' in Doan
(ed.), The Lesbian Postmodern, pp.
67–84; 'The Labours of Love,
Analysing Perverse Desire: An
Interrogation of Teresa de Lauretis's
The Practice of Love', Differences,
Vol. 6 Nos 2 and 3, Summer–Fall,
1994b, pp. 274–95.

27. Jonathan Dollimore, Sexual
Dissidence: Augustine to Wilde,
Freud to Foucault (Oxford: Oxford
University Press, 1991); and 'The
Cultural Politics of Perversion:
Augustine, Shakespeare, Freud,
Foucault' in Joe Bristow (ed.), Sexual
Sameness (London and New York:
Routledge, 1992), pp. 9–25.

28. Eve Sedgwick, Epistemology of the
Closet (Berkeley, Los Angeles:
University of California Press, 1990),
and 'Queer Performativity: Henry
James's The Art of the Novel', GLQ,
Vol. 1 Pt. 1, Spring 1993, pp. 1–16.

29. I am thinking specifically of the
work undertaken by Judith
Williamson; see, for example, her
books, Decoding Advertisements:
Ideology and Meaning in Advertising
(London and New York: Marion
Boyars, 1992, first published in
1978), and Consuming Passions: The
Dynamics of Popular Culture
(London and New York: Marion
Boyars, 1986, first published in
1980).

30. See de Lauretis, The Practice of
Love; and Parveen Adams, 'The
Three (Dis)Graces', New
Formations: A Journal of
Culture/Theory/Politics, Perversity
Issue, No. 19, Spring 1993, pp.
131–8, and The Emptiness of the
Image: Psychoanalysis and Sexual
Differences (London and New York:
Routledge, 1996).

31. Lynne Pearce and Jackie Stacey (eds),
Romance Revisited (London:
Lawrence and Wishart, 1995).

32. Christine McEwen and Sue
O'Sullivan (eds), Out The Other
Side: Contemporary Lesbian Writing
(London: Virago, 1988).

33. Sue Cartledge and Joanna Ryan
(eds), Sex and Love: New Thoughts
on Old Contradictions (London: The
Women's Press, 1987, first published
in 1983).

34. See, for example, Elizabeth Wilson,
'I'll Climb the Stairway to Heaven:
Lesbianism in the Seventies' in ibid.,
pp. 180–95.

35. Ann Snitow (ed.), Desire: The
Politics of Sexuality (London:
Virago, 1983).

36. Carol Vance (ed.), Pleasure and
Danger: Exploring Female Sexuality
(London: Routledge and Kegan Paul,
1984).

37. Gabrielle Griffin (ed.), Outwrite:
Lesbianism and Popular Culture
(London: Pluto Press, 1993).

38. Liz Gibbs (ed.), Daring to Dissent:
Lesbian Culture from Margin to
Mainstream (London and New York:
Cassell, 1994).

39. Budge and Hamer (eds), The Good,
the Bad and the Gorgeous.

40. Tamsin Wilton (ed.), Immortal,
Invisible: Lesbians and the Moving
Image (London and New York:
Routledge, 1995).

41. Stein (ed.), Sisters, Sexperts, Queers.

42. Corey K. Creekmur and Alexander
Doty (eds), Out in Culture: Gay,
Lesbian and Queer Essays on
Popular Culture (London: Cassell,
1995).

2

'Doctor, Doctor, There's a Dyke in My Theory!' Gay Master Narrative and the Unqueering of the Lesbian

Introduction

The recent popularization of lesbian identity has occurred in a broad range of contexts within the mainstream media. This has become apparent both in elements of lifestyle, such as popular media representation and fashion trends,[1] and also in a growing body of theory about lesbian identity which parallels the popular domain. In order to understand how lesbian identities are produced in a specific lesbian star/fan relationship, and how conventional codes of masculinity are re-deployed in this context, it is important to develop a theoretical framework within which to examine properly the implications and consequences of this project.

The theories I chart in this chapter all engage with the relationship between sexuality and western cultural formations and epistemologies, and are all critiques of heterosexual power. However, I aim to highlight why some of these theories foreclose the analysis of lesbian culture and identity, and how others, by contrast, offer ways to interrogate the specificities of lesbian identity formation, and lesbian cultural and social practices.

Here, then, I will analyse how a specific academic forum for studying lesbian identity and culture has developed over the past few years, discussing the work of Judith Butler,[2] Teresa de Lauretis[3] and Elizabeth Grosz.[4] These theorists have developed arguments about how lesbian identity is constructed through the constitutive effects of social and cultural practices, but also consistently imply that lesbianism is a 'lived identity', and that lesbians are often oppressed by established modes of domination. I argue, along with these theorists, that lesbian identity and culture are in one sense constituted by and through the effects of social and cultural practices – i.e. that I do not work with the idea of a 'lesbian essence'. However, like these theorists, I do not want to deny the consistent identification of those who, in Butler's terms, 'appear under the sign of lesbian'.[5] In other words, I approach with caution both the essentialist and the constructionist views that have marked the theorization of lesbian identity. Further, I want to understand this tension in relation to the lesbian stardom and fandom that frames this analysis.

However, before examining recent theories of sexuality in depth, it is important to understand how the academic space within which Butler, de Lauretis and Grosz have published, has opened up over the past few years. Significantly, increased theoretical attention to the question of lesbian identity has, in part, been due to the development of 'queer theory'. Queer theory has developed from a lesbian and gay theoretical perspective – a perspective which has seen radical potential in the re-appropriation of homophobic labelling, within which context the formerly negative connotation ascribed to the term 'queer' has been turned on its head and flaunted at heterosexual culture.

In this chapter, therefore, I will also examine the work of Eve Sedgwick[6] and Jonathan Dollimore,[7] whom I call 'queer theorists', and who have both published work in the area of sexuality from the perspective of literary theory. I shall argue that their theories prioritize gay male identity and culture, and thus do not allow for a discussion of lesbian identity and, further, even though writing from post-structuralist camps and about the social process, their theories also employ 'queer' to mean an *essence*.

Despite the limits of the queer theory I describe in this chapter, I believe it is possible to use the notion of queer in different ways in relation to cultural production and consumption practices, which do not necessarily prioritize a gay male identity, or which see queerness or perversion as an essence. Whilst cautious about using the term 'queer' in any way myself, to use queer as a verb – to 'queer a text', for example – may hold transformative potential.

In my view the theories of Butler, de Lauretis and Grosz should not be termed 'queer'. This is because of major differences in the mode of theorization employed by Sedgwick and Dollimore in comparison to that of Butler, de Lauretis and Grosz. The theories of Butler, de Lauretis and

Grosz produce possibilities for discussing cultural practices significant to the constitution of *lesbian* identity; possibilities that, I suggest, are not offered in the theories of Sedgwick and Dollimore. Thus my arguments about the resignification of masculinity in the context of lesbian cultural practices will be constructed in relation to the theoretical possibilities that I will open up here, through critiques both of queer theory and more specific theories around lesbian culture and identity.

Queer Street (A Trip Up)

Jonathan Dollimore and the 'Perverse Dynamic'

Jonathan Dollimore's book, *Sexual Dissidence: Augustine to Wilde, Freud to Foucault*, is a study of various literary texts, a general summary of which appears in an article he wrote, entitled 'The Cultural Politics of Perversion: Augustine, Shakespeare, Freud, Foucault'.[8] In this article the key arguments which define him as a queer theorist become clear. For convenience, therefore, I will refer to this latter article throughout my examination of his theory.

Dollimore's work is central to the development of queer theory in Britain, and his analysis of homosexuality and literary texts centres around his notion of the 'perverse dynamic'. Citing Freud and Foucault,[9] Dollimore sees perversion as *endemic* to modern society, using the conceptual premise of 'the other' existing within 'the same'. Using the narrative of 'The Fall', in which evil is seen to be a *quality of* good/God, Dollimore refers to perversion as fundamentally related 'internally to just those things it threatens':[10]

> Somehow the perverse is inextricably rooted in the true and authentic, while being, in spite of (or rather because of) that connection, also the utter contradiction of it. This paradox begins to suggest why perversion, theological or sexual, is so often conceived as *at once utterly alien to, and yet mysteriously inherent within* the true and authentic.[11]

In this confusing conceptual loop Dollimore describes the paradox of the other existing within the same by highlighting the paradox of the other existing within the same.

Dollimore then goes on to develop a notion of 'proximity' in relation to this model of the perverse dynamic, arguing that negation/deviation 'erupts from *within* that which it negates',[12] to be displaced onto the subordinate side of the binary division. He suggests: '*Proximity, therefore, is the enabling condition of a displacement which in turn marks the "same" as radically "other"*.'[13] As Dollimore uses the God/man binary as an exemplary division here, he is able to assert that the original pervert was not Satan, but God.

In an analysis of queer popular culture, *Making Things Perfectly Queer*, Alexander Doty makes similar claims about queer: 'Queer readings aren't "alternative" readings, wishful or wilful misreadings, or "reading too much into things" readings. They result from the recognition and articulation of the complex range of queerness that has been in popular culture texts and their audiences all along.'[14]

The implication in both Doty and Dollimore, then, is that 'queerness' is a quality which exists *within* a text, a person or a concept, which queer readers, or indeed queer theorists, are able to read *as* queer. Here, queer theory is reductionist, as perversion or queerness is viewed as an intrinsic property of a text – which may be read by a 'true' queer reader (whoever that may be). Dollimore, for example, draws the production of meaning down to a conceptual level that elides the possibility for an individual to be a subject or agent in the social field; indeed, according to Dollimore *proximity* is the agent that enables displacement.

Although Dollimore writes from an anti-essentialist position, I believe his analysis *is* essentialist because he maintains that perversion is an intrinsic and structuring element of modern western society. Perhaps anticipating such a critique, he makes the following qualification: 'Perversion subverts not in the recovery of a pre-social libido, or an original plenitude, but as a dynamic intrinsic to social process.'[15] However, this is simply concealing an essentialist move behind a smokescreen of social constructionism.[16] Now, I am not arguing that essentialist reasoning is *always* reactionary; indeed I do not wish to suggest that essentialism is necessarily 'bad' or that constructionism, on the other hand, is necessarily 'good';[17] however, the effect of Dollimore's essentialism is that it produces a deeply sexist and, ironically, homophobic theory. Further, in Dollimore's theory of perversion, essentialism anchors a circular dynamic of 'the perverse', which is also the 'true' (the 'other' which is also the 'same'); caught up in a web of conceptual reductionism the 'perverse' rests quietly on the side of the dominant order and lacks transformative potential.

I would argue that transformative potential depends on contextualized consumption practices and not on the assertion of a universalizing rule;

that meanings of texts are only created, or produced, in the relationship between text and reader and within specific contexts of experience. Dollimore's and Doty's accounts are tied to a latent propensity *for* perversion in society, and Dollimore's theory, in particular, prioritizes a male homosexual identity through his discussion of the possible subversion of heterosexual cultural privilege. This kind of queer analysis undercuts the potential for subversive meanings inherent in modes of consumption by lesbians.

Eve Sedgwick and male homosexuality

As we have seen, Dollimore prioritizes the homosexual/heterosexual distinction in his queer analysis. In *Epistemology of the Closet*, Eve Sedgwick prioritized the same homosexual/heterosexual binary as a model for understanding contemporary western culture, arguing that male desire is central to western culture:

> *Epistemology of the Closet* proposes that many of the major nodes of thought and knowledges in twentieth-century Western culture as a whole are structured – indeed fractured – by a chronic, now endemic crisis of homo/heterosexual definition, indicatively male, dating from the end of the nineteenth century.[18]

In this book Sedgwick takes the Foucauldian theory of sexuality as axiomatic,[19] explaining that her perspective is one of 'modern gay and antihomophobic theory'.[20] She suggests that the homo/hetero dualism is as important in organizing western society as 'the more traditionally visible cruxes of gender, class and race',[21] and provides a detailed list of other binaries which are interrelated with, and implied by, this particular dyad:

> I'll argue that the now chronic modern crisis of homo/heterosexual definition has affected our culture through its ineffaceable marking particularly of the categories secrecy/disclosure, knowledge/ignorance, private/public, masculine/feminine, majority/minority, innocence/ initiation, natural/artificial, new/old, discipline/terrorism, canonic/ noncanonic, wholeness/decadence, urbane/provincial, domestic/foreign, health/illness, same/different, active/passive, in/out, cognition/paranoia, art/kitsch, utopia/apocalypse, sincerity/sentimentality, and voluntarity/ addiction.[22]

Sedgwick systematically analyses several texts, such as *Billy Budd*,[23] and suggests that all the above dualisms may be pinpointed in the texts, and deconstructed via the homosexuality/heterosexuality dichotomy and the prioritization of gay male desire.

Sedgwick uses the framework of literary theory to explore the 'performative' aspects of texts, and their 'reader-relations', as sites of definitional creation, violence and rupture. She argues that the relations of 'The Closet' have potential to reveal the nature of the concept of performativity, particularly through interrogating such binarisms as known/unknown. Sedgwick's work is deconstructive in that it clarifies the ways in which cultural knowledges and beliefs around male homosexuality are discursively reproduced throughout various realms of epistemology (the binaries quoted above). However, Sedgwick's arguments are deconstructive in a circular fashion, in that they are also *re*constructive – she examines binaries in order to analyse how they are reproduced, just as Dollimore describes the paradox that is *the other within the same* by highlighting how *the other within the same* is a paradox.

Sedgwick does not reread Freud's theory of the 'polymorphously perverse', so characteristic of Dollimore's study; however, she does imply the same thing as Dollimore – namely, that a structuring male *homosexuality* inhabits us all (the 'other' exists within the 'same') and consequently that female agency is only possible via the adoption of a male homosexual subjectivity and desire. This centrality of male homosexuality in Sedgwick's theory is apparent in her assertion that homophobes may be described as homosexuals. In her analysis of the 'homosexual' character Claggart in *Billy Budd*, Sedgwick argues that the ambiguity in the text about his sexual preference, coupled with his 'depravity', class him as homosexual:

> What *was* ... the matter with the master at arms? Claggart is depraved because he is, in his desires, a pervert, of a sort that by 1891 had names in several taxonomic systems although scarcely yet, in English, the name 'homosexual'; or, second, that Claggart is depraved not because of the male-directed nature of his desire, here seen as natural or innocuous, but, rather, because he feels toward his own desires only terror and loathing (call this 'phobia'). The relation between these two possible answers – that Claggart is depraved because homosexual, or, alternatively depraved because homophobic – is of course an odd

problem. Suffice it here to say that either could qualify him for, and certainly neither would disqualify him from, a designation like 'homosexual'.[24]

Sedgwick's dense yet non-committal theorizations in this passage do not, for me, disguise the implications of her words. Indeed, it is my understanding that Claggart's sexual ambiguity simply reflects the politically dubious premise of Sedgwick's own theory – that homosexuality is a foundational identity which inhabits us all. Although from an entirely different theoretical position, and with a different emphasis in terms of gender, Sedgwick's conclusion is remarkably similar to the notion of the 'lesbian continuum' suggested by Adrienne Rich in her now historic essay, 'Compulsory Heterosexuality and Lesbian Existence'.[25] Although Rich notes that there are specific forms of lesbian culture which involve a sexual element, she also, in one sense, undercuts the power of lesbian-specific cultural practices by suggesting that all relations between women are a form of lesbian existence along a continuum. This argument effectively rejects the specificity of lesbian identity by suggesting that all women have the potential to identify as 'lesbians' of one kind or another.[26]

In an article which extends her arguments about performativity, 'Queer Performativity', Sedgwick explains how the concept of 'shame' is central to understanding the constitution of homosexuality, using it as a bridging force between the binary division normal/queer. Discussing the relationship of performativity to queer theory, Sedgwick argues that performativity is a very queer concept: 'The stretch between theatrical and deconstructive meanings of "performativity" seems to span the polarities of, at either extreme, the *extroversion* of the actor, the *introversion* of the signifier.'[27] Here, Sedgwick supplies a model of binary opposition (introversion/ extroversion) which structures her subsequent arguments about 'queer performativity'. Thus she makes sense of queer performativity through an understanding of a strict binary division.

In this article she cites J. L. Austin's example of performativity – the location of the wedding ceremony phrase 'I do' in the first-person singular present indicative active. She then argues that the formulation 'Shame on you' has greater potential for a queer reading than 'I do', as the phrase has no 'I' as the subject of the utterance and no verb in the utterance. Thus Sedgwick situates the utterance of 'Shame on you' within an understanding of performativity which relates to those 'who self-identify as queer'. Existing at the periphery of subjectivity, these shamed beings hence threaten the subjectivity of the absent 'I' who casts the shame:

> the very grammatical truncation of 'Shame on you' marks it as the product of a history out of which an I, now withdrawn, is projecting shame toward another I, an I deferred, that has yet and with difficulty to come into being, if at all, in the place of the shamed second person. The verblessness of this particular performative, then, implies a first person whose singular/plural status, whose past/present/future status, and indeed whose agency/passivity can only be questioned rather than presumed.[28]

Sedgwick is suggesting that 'Shame' is the 'disruptive moment' that *constitutes* the queer self, arguing that queerness is identifiable through 'Shame', and, moreover, that the 'Shamed' threaten the homophobic persecutors. She believes that those (or we) who are shamed, whilst being shamed, are effecting a deconstruction of the power that shames. But should we not, rather, be addressing the way in which the silencing, and subordination, of people who are 'shamed' takes place in particular cultural settings? I would argue that different cultural contexts of shaming determine whether or not the person who is shamed either threatens the subjectivity of the shamer (as Sedgwick suggests *always* happens), or is merely subordinated by the shamer. Surely Sedgwick underestimates the power of homophobia if she insists that being shamed is intrinsically threatening to the dominating perpetrator of that shame?

The theories of Dollimore and Sedgwick are clearly problematic, as their universalizing assumptions are held fast through highly abstracted and conceptual logic. One could in fact argue that these theories are almost commensurate with psychoanalytic reductionism, as they are structured by the circular inevitability of the primacy of *masculine desire* in their attempts to subvert or trouble heterosexual regulation. Hence I reject the theories of both Sedgwick and Dollimore, and also psychoanalytic theory, because they turn on this *a priori* male desire.

Querying Queer

Certain theorists working from the perspective of lesbian sexuality have criticized queer theories. In 'Queer Theory and the War of the Sexes' Mary McIntosh regards Dollimore's work on sexual dissidence as 'perhaps the most sustained and interesting work of queer theory'.[29] However, she extends a warning for lesbians or feminists using queer theory. Although explaining that, as in the construction of the gay man, the construction of the lesbian has been sexual and transgressive, she asserts that, conversely, queer theory 'should not forget that the heterosexuality in terms of which we are defined as other is a highly gendered one, so that our otherness and the forms and meanings of our dissidence are also gendered',[30] and goes on to urge feminists to agitate for gender awareness in queer theory. McIntosh's response to queer theory is similar to my reservations about the kinds of queer theory offered by Dollimore and Sedgwick.

At the beginning of *Lesbians Talk Queer Notions*[31] Cherry Smyth documents the social context within which queer politics developed in Britain and the USA in the early 1990s, and how 'queer' became such a key word in the politics of sexuality. Highlighting the rise of Queer Nation in the USA and the direct action group OutRage! in Britain, she also emphasizes how identification as queer stretches beyond the membership of such campaigning groups, signalling a general dissatisfaction with lesbian and gay politics of the past.

Smyth claims that the AIDS 'epidemic' led to an increase in victimization and gave rise to much anger amongst gays and lesbians, fuelling a renewed sense of disenfranchisement and complacency in the younger members of the community. Within this context, she argues, SILENCE = DEATH became the password of a new generation of 'queers' who challenged the silencing of AIDS which had occurred through government neglect and renewed homophobia in both the law and on the street. Thus she maintains that the 'cry for safer sex information, research and drugs to fight the AIDS epidemic expanded into a campaign against all homophobic oppression. An urgent sense of mortality inspired the rejection of respectability and discretion.'[32] However, Smyth also problematizes the notion of queer in terms of sexism and racism, and highlights the mistrust felt by many oppressed social groups towards a supposed 'new age' of inclusive co-operation under the political aegis of 'queer'.

The tendency of queer politics to be a predominantly white male movement also relates to what is currently being termed 'queer theory' in an academic context. 'Queer theory' is used to describe both recent work in the wide category of 'studies of sexuality' and any mode of theorization which employs an understanding of 'perversity' or 'abjection'[33] and is challenging to normative categories of identity. However, this broad context is misleading in its use of the term 'queer'. It is a shifting signifier, and 'queer' seems to mean many different things – it could refer to a text, a reading of a text, a theory, a mode of political action, or, as I have already suggested, it may be used as a verb: 'to queer'. Some texts, theories or actions may be said to *be* queer, whereas queer theorists argue that texts can become subversive through queer rereadings which seem to locate a queer 'element' in the text.

On the whole, there seems to be great confusion as to what constitutes either a queer text, a queer theory or the location of queer itself. Helen (charles), in an article entitled 'Queer Nigger: Theorizing "White" Activism',[34] has discussed the definition of queer in relation to the potential racism, sexism and homophobia within the concept. There are undoubtedly important differences, but also to some extent interconnections, between queer theory and queer politics. As McIntosh writes: 'Queer politics ... is rooted (albeit rather shadowily) in a queer theory that is deconstructive of categories and subjectivities.'[35] In *Bodies that Matter* Judith Butler writes of 'queer':

> The term 'queer' has operated as one linguistic practice whose purpose has been the shaming of the subject it names, or, rather, the producing of the subject *through* that shaming interpellation. 'Queer' derives its force precisely through the repeated invocation by which it has become linked to accusation, pathologization, insult.[36]

However, I would argue that one of the differences between queer theory and queer politics is that, where queer theorists attempt to deconstruct categories, queer activists organize around identity politics in order to take part in political actions. In other words, and perhaps paradoxically, the goal of queer politics is to attract a significant number of 'lesbian' and 'gay' activists. In this way, queer politics relies on the *rhetoric* of identity politics in order to appeal predominantly to lesbians and gay men for the ironic purpose of trying to deconstruct the very identities it attempts to hail.[37]

The queer theories of Sedgwick and Dollimore sit within this context of the reconstruction/deconstruction of identity. The problem with queer activism, as (charles) and Smyth have noted, is that it is often a predominantly white male movement, serving predominantly white male interests. This exclusion of lesbian interests, and the interests of those subordinated through racism, is, I believe, reproduced in the theories of Dollimore and Sedgwick, as they exclude the weighty contribution made by feminist and post-colonial theory[38] to cultural theory in recent years. The theories of Dollimore and Sedgwick are *emblematic* of the queer movement in academia, and the problems I have highlighted in their theories should lead us to question whether we should be using a queer label at all when theorizing about lesbian identity.

Theorizing Lesbian Identity

The theories put forward by Judith Butler,[39] Teresa de Lauretis[40] and Elizabeth Grosz[41] raise important questions about ways of examining lesbian culture and identity, and lead us to ask just how much the strand of queer theory, represented by Dollimore and Sedgwick, has to offer studies of lesbianism in general. It is thus important to understand at which points Butler, de Lauretis and Grosz intersect, and, also how my analysis relates to their respective positions.

Even though she considers the discursive construction of lesbian identity, Butler still wants the meaning of the term 'lesbian' to remain unclear. In an article about the problem of identity, entitled 'Imitation and Gender Insubordination', Butler argues:

> I'm not at ease with 'lesbian theories, gay theories', for ... identity categories tend to be instruments of regulatory regimes. ... That is not to say that I will not appear under the sign of lesbian, but that I would like to have it permanently unclear what precisely that sign signifies.[42]

By 'sign' I understand Butler to mean a lesbian identification which contributes to and partakes of a lesbian culture in different and variable contexts. This definition of lesbian thus makes it possible to discuss the empirical data that I have collected from self-defined lesbian fans of the lesbian idols Martina and kd, and to produce discourses about lesbian identity, lesbian identification and lesbian culture.

In using lesbian identity as the starting point for my analysis rather than the problematization of identity *per se* (as Butler does), I examine how the construction of this identity takes place. What is clear is that people do self-identify as lesbians (as Butler herself notes, and indeed *does*). Therefore, my analysis certainly questions the notion of identity itself, but also stresses, with reference to a specific case study which examines consumption practices in the lesbian star/fan relationship,[43] how and why identifying in certain ways is important.

Also central to my examination of lesbian consumption practices is the way heterosexual identity and heterosexual culture operate contradictorily, and how challenges to heterosexual knowledges may be articulated at such points of contradiction. As I noted above, Martina and kd, and the fans whose experiences are contained in this book, all 'appear under the sign of lesbian.'[44] I will suggest that at specific conjunctures (of, for example, identification, experience, consumption) such an 'appearance' often highlights the points at which dominant heterosexual identities are both contradictory and unstable.

To help me in this, my theoretical framework will draw on the notion of signification. I will argue that the consumption of lesbian idols by lesbian consumers redeploys the representational codes of heterosexual masculinity in a specific context of lesbian identity formation. Such an argument demands that we examine how sex and gender are lived and interpreted in relation to the question of sexuality, and thus, how sex and gender are reproduced in these sites of lesbian consumption.

In *Technologies of Gender: Essays on Theory, Film and Fiction*, Teresa de Lauretis has noted how sex and gender are categorizations of identity that constitute the subject through cultural signification. Although her book centres on the representation of sex and gender in relation to cinema and feminist theory, her theoretical position in this book is similar to mine. She argues:

> gender is not a sex, a state of nature, but the representation of each individual in terms of a particular social relation which pre-exists the individual and is predicated on the conceptual and rigid (structural) opposition of two biological sexes. This conceptual structure is what feminist social scientists have designated 'the sex-gender system'.[45]

De Lauretis goes on to discuss this sex-gender system in relation to semiotics – the representation of meaning:

> The sex-gender system, in short, is both a sociocultural construct and a semiotic apparatus, a system of representation which assigns meaning (identity, value, prestige, location in kinship, status in the social hierarchy, etc.) to individuals within the society. If gender representations are social positions which carry differential meanings, then for someone to be represented and to represent oneself as male or as female implies the assumption of the whole of those meaning

effects. Thus, the proposition that the representation of gender is its construction, each term being at once the product and the process of the other, can be restated more accurately: the construction of gender is both the product and the process of its representation.[46]

I will examine, as does de Lauretis, how identities are produced and sustained, and how dominations are either secured or resisted through strategies of signification in relation to representations. I want to suggest, therefore, that representation and identity are bound up in an interactive manoeuvre. I also want to examine how privileging meaning systems may be troubled by the manner in which representations of lesbian identity are consumed by lesbians. De Lauretis highlights the importance of analysing the specific practices of subordinated individuals, and the destabilizing effect this can have on the construction of gender – an effect she calls 'gender trauma'. She argues that a critique of discourses concerning gender by feminist theorists is vital in order to create 'new spaces of discourse, to rewrite cultural narratives, and to define the terms of another perspective – a view from "elsewhere".' [47] She continues:

> ... that 'elsewhere' is not some mythic distant past or some utopian future history: it is the elsewhere of discourse here and now, the blind spots, or the space-off, of its representations ... spaces in the margins of hegemonic discourses, social spaces carved in the interstices of institutions and in the chinks and cracks of the power-knowledge apparati. And it is there that the terms of a different construction of gender can be posed – terms that do have effect and take hold at the level of subjectivity and self-representation: in the micropolitical practices of daily life and daily resistances that afford both agency and sources of power or empowering investments: and in the cultural productions of women, feminists, which inscribe that movement in and out of ideology, that crossing back and forth of the boundaries – and of the limits – of sexual difference(s).[48]

The Trouble with Gender

Judith Butler's book *Gender Trouble* was published at a crucial time, when the representation of lesbian identity in the Anglo-American mainstream media started to outgrow a short-term flirtation and became more of a cultural trend. Commenting on the theoretical arenas of psychoanalysis, feminism and identity, Butler examines the interconnection between such theories and the issue of lesbian identity.[49]

Her ground-breaking argument in *Gender Trouble* may signal the emergence of a specifically lesbian strand of 'queer theory', but in my view this book departs sufficiently from queer theory not to be referred to as 'queer' at all. Thus, even though the works of Butler and de Lauretis are often cited as queer interventions in the academic field, I would suggest that to call these writers 'queer theorists' is to imply that their theories are organized around the kind of reductive framework used by Dollimore and Sedgwick.

In *Gender Trouble* Butler works with an analytical model which interconnects feminist and Foucauldian theory to discuss the binary structure which governs the organization of sex, gender and desire in western culture. Throughout her discussions she critiques various feminist theorists who have attempted to dislodge the structures of a masculinist and heterosexist signifying economy. Regarding the use of semiology, and in particular her assertion that the notion of 'performativity' remains central to any understanding of the reproduction of identity, Butler's model is quite similar to the work of Sedgwick. However, on closer inspection, it becomes clear that employing a notion of performativity to discuss cultural relations is not *necessarily* subversive of heterosexual domination and male privilege; performativity *per se* cannot ensure that queer theory is a radical intervention into dominant modes of thought. Butler's persistent awareness of this problem further undermines the credibility of Sedgwick's work.

Butler's analysis of drag in *Gender Trouble* is also important to the study of lesbian identity, as she challenges the authenticity and the 'givenness' of the heterosexual regime of sexual and gender difference and the subordination of lesbian identity, posing the crucial question: 'Is drag the imitation of gender, or does it dramatize the signifying gestures through which gender itself is established?'[50]

Butler's overall thesis in *Gender Trouble* questions the pre-existence of sex categories over gender categories, maintaining, rather, that these two formulations of identity are the interrelated effects of regulatory regimes of heterosexual power:

If the immutable character of sex is contested, perhaps this construct called 'sex' is as culturally constructed as gender; indeed, perhaps it was always already gender, with the consequence that the distinction between sex and gender turns out to be no distinction at all.[51]

Subsequently, Butler argues that gender is 'performative', that it reiterates the identity it is purported to be ('iteration' is like saying a name: a name reconstitutes the person or thing it denotes via an act of iteration or speech). In this sense gender, she argues, 'does itself'; she also suggests that there is no pre-existent subject called a 'man' or a 'woman' who 'does' or 'has' their gender. This position has led to much confusion, however, in the analyses of lesbian identity that have succeeded Butler's *Gender Trouble*. Whilst representation has a constitutive role in identity and culture formation, there are also historical, political and social continuums to take into consideration.

We must understand that this idea of gender reiteration does not necessarily signify a subversive manoeuvre. Butler clarifies the regulatory function that structures such acts of gender reiteration, claiming:

> gender is not a noun, but neither is it a set of free-floating attributes, for we have seen that the substantive effect of gender is performatively produced and compelled by the regulatory practices of gender coherence. Hence, within the inherited discourse of the metaphysics of substance, gender proves to be performative – that is, constituting the identity it is purported to be. In this sense, gender is always a doing, though not a doing by a subject who might be said to preexist the deed.[52]

In questioning the existence of the 'doer' behind the gender, Butler also problematizes the notion of the 'subject'. In particular she argues that Monique Wittig's theory of lesbian identity posits 'the lesbian' as a third gender that promises to transcend the binary restriction on sex imposed by the system of compulsory heterosexuality. However, Butler argues that within Wittig's schema the subject, inscribed as masculine by the patriarchal 'symbolic' (the idea of the symbolic is taken from Lacanian theory), is not criticized, as she places her 'lesbian' within the conceptual rubric of subject relations: 'As a subject who can realize concrete universality through freedom, Wittig's lesbian confirms rather than contests the normative promise of humanist ideals premised on the metaphysics of substance.'[53]

Having created a conceptual backdrop from which to fully interrogate gender and sex through the notions of subjectivity and identity, Butler develops a critique of psychoanalytic theory, asking questions that hold immense significance for any theoretical analysis of lesbianism. Examining the theories of both Freud and Lacan, she argues that Freud insists on the notion of 'primary dispositions' which subsequently determine the success or failure of the Oedipus complex in girls and boys. Butler is intrigued by Freud's assertion, especially where, considering disposition in general, he ponders: '"whatever that may consist in"'[54] In relation to the Oedipus complex and the primary dispositions, she asks:

> how do we identify a 'feminine' or a 'masculine' disposition at the outset? By what traces is it known, and to what extent do we assume a 'feminine' or a 'masculine' disposition as a precondition of a heterosexual object choice? In other words, to what extent do we read the desire for the father as evidence of a feminine disposition only because we begin, despite the postulation of a primary bisexuality, with a heterosexual matrix for desire?[55]

She maintains that Freud's notion of primary 'bisexual' dispositions is regulated by a compulsory heterosexuality: 'The conceptualization of bisexuality in terms of *dispositions*, feminine and masculine, which have heterosexual aims as their intentional correlates, suggests that for Freud *bisexuality is the coincidence of two heterosexual desires within a single psyche.*'[56] Significantly, Butler uses Freud's idea of primary dispositions to highlight how psychoanalytic discourse hides its own modes of operation. She suggests that the melancholia of gender identification in Freud which 'answers' the Oedipal drama should be understood as '...the internalization of an interior moral directive which gains its structure and energy from an externally enforced taboo'.[57] Freud's 'dispositions' are brought in to conceal the way that the Oedipal drama operates by virtue of a law that is produced externally. Butler goes on to claim that the aim of this disguising strategy is to exclude the production of alternative understandings of culture. She maintains that the 'law of the father'

> [Instates] itself as the principle of logical contiguity in a narrative of causal relations which takes psychic facts as its point of departure, this configuration of the law forecloses the possibility of a more radical genealogy into the cultural origins of sexuality and power relations.[58]

Butler also complains of circular production/repression in Lacanian theory,[59] claiming that Lacan instigates similar regulatory categories of gender and sex, and so reproduces a heterosexual telos for desire. Butler asserts that Lacan's theory contains a heterosexual reductionism (a reductionism reminiscent of the queer theories of Dollimore and Sedgwick), where all desire originates from a masculine heterosexual subject position; even if the desiring subject is a lesbian she is said to be enacting a masquerade of male heterosexual desire:

> This is the predicament produced by a matrix that accounts for all desire for women by subjects of whatever sex or gender as originating in a masculine, heterosexual position. The libido-as-masculine is the source from which all possible sexuality is presumed to come.[60]

Butler notes that for Lacan there is no discursive reality; in Lacanian theory the fundamental split that renders the subject internally divided and that establishes the duality of the sexes is an *effect* of paternal law, and not a pre-existent condition on which the law acts. Further, for Lacan, identification, and the drama of either being the phallus (women) or having the phallus (men) is phantasmic, and as such bears witness to a symbolic law of the father which resists a connection to pre-existent dispositions or drives. However, Butler is dubious about the consequence of Lacan's argument, because he reinscribes binary sex and gender differences: 'That the language of physiology or disposition does not appear here is welcome news, but binary restrictions nevertheless still operate to frame and formulate sexuality and delimit in advance the forms of its resistance to the real.'[61]

Butler's critiques of Freud and Lacan exemplify her concern with interrogating the meta-narrative of psychoanalysis, which is a pervasive theoretical reiteration of heterosexualized binary categories of sex and gender. The overall aim of *Gender Trouble* is, then, to re-imagine 'gender' by examining the culturally reiterative performativities of sex and gender through which heterosexual restrictions are produced and yet may also be undermined and dislodged. Using the example of language to highlight how heterosexually restrictive genders may be challenged, she deploys one of the strategies of early queer theory, suggesting: 'The terms *queens, butches, femmes, girls*, even the parodic reappropriation of *dyke, queer*, and *fag* redeploy and destabilize the categories of sex and the originally derogatory categories for homosexual identity.'[62] The idea of re-appropriating terms inscribed with negative meanings by heterosexual discourse is one of the generative moves of queer and, citing Butler, is a good way to illustrate how such a strategy developed out of lesbian and gay culture, only to be tied to male homosexuality in the theories of Dollimore and Sedgwick.

Butler further examines how a visual parodic performativity of gender may resist heterosexual discourse:

> The notion of an original or primary gender identity is often parodied within the cultural practices of drag, cross-dressing, and the sexual stylization of butch/femme identities. ... *In imitating gender, drag implicitly reveals the imitative structure of gender itself – as well as its contingency.*[63]

But she also issues a warning: 'Parody by itself is not subversive, and there must be a way to understand what makes certain kinds of parodic repetitions effectively disruptive, truly troubling, and which repetitions become domesticated and recirculated as instruments of cultural hegemony.'[64] Butler's assertion that the subversive potential of reappropriative manoeuvres, such as drag, is *never guaranteed* helps us to understand how the theories of Dollimore and Sedgwick may reproduce a hierarchical division between gays and lesbians at the level of theory.

Gender Trouble is a radical analysis which makes us look closely at the cultural fabric of western society, and yet it remains cautious about the possibilities for resistance to forms of heterosexual domination. What should be taken from this book is an understanding that hegemonic heterosexual practices, far from being cohesive, are open to continuous rearticulation, but that this rearticulation must take place in specific and contextualized manoeuvres based on cultural and social practice. Indeed, Butler is keen to assert that what we need is a rigorous understanding of how to theorize lesbian cultural practices:

> If subversion is possible, it will be a subversion from within the terms of the law, through the possibilities that emerge when the law turns against itself and spawns unexpected permutations of itself. The culturally constructed body will then be liberated, neither to its 'natural' past, nor to its original pleasures, but to an open future of cultural possibilities.[65]

Butler's subsequent book, *Bodies that Matter*, was an attempt to clarify her arguments in *Gender Trouble*, and also to extend these arguments along a number of different trajectories. In this book she focuses on several literary and film texts: Plato's *Timaeus*, Freud's 'On Narcissism', writings by Lacan, stories by Willa Cather, Nella Larsen's novella *Passing* and Jennie Livingston's film *Paris is Burning*. Throughout her readings of these texts her aim is to specify how 'regulatory norms of "sex"' work performatively in order to 'constitute the materiality of bodies', 'to materialize the body's sex' and 'to materialize sexual difference in the service of the consolidation of the heterosexual imperative'.[66]

The problematic issue of subjectivity is very much at the centre of her project in this book. Arguing that because subjects are formed in an exclusionary matrix, 'abject beings' are also produced which 'form the constitutive outside to the domain of the subject',[67] she also forewarns that any attempt to produce feminist cultural theory that will dislodge or trouble diverse forms of regulation and domination runs the risk of reproducing a pre-existent subject *of* domination without a critique of the means by which subjectivity is established:

> if gender is constructed, it is not necessarily constructed by an 'I' or a 'we' who stands before that construction in any spatial or temporal sense of 'before'. Indeed, it is unclear that there can be an 'I' or 'we' who has not been submitted, subjected to gender, where gendering is, among other things, the differentiating relations by which speaking subjects come into being. Subjected to gender, but subjectivated by gender, the 'I' neither precedes nor follows the process of this gendering, but emerges only within and as the matrix of gender relations themselves.[68]

To understand Butler's theory of the subject as a gendered process, it is useful to reiterate de Lauretis's argument in *Technologies of Gender*: where Butler suggests that the subject is formed in a matrix of gender relations, de Lauretis ties this process of gendering to representation, an argument that is central to my thesis about the constitution of lesbian identity and meanings of gender and sex in the lesbian star/fan relationship. In the next section I will go on to examine de Lauretis's book *The Practice of Love*, which specifically concentrates on the question of lesbian identity.

Teresa de Lauretis and the Practice of Love

In her analysis of lesbian cultural practices in *The Practice of Love* de Lauretis attempts to articulate lesbianism in relation to Freudian psychoanalysis.[69] It is important to clarify this interconnection from both a feminist and a lesbian point of view, and to analyse the consequences of her arguments in this book, because, as I argued above in relation to the theories of Dollimore and Sedgwick, many understandings of queer theory are premised on problematic psychoanalytic principles which prioritize the subversive potential of male homosexual desire.

De Lauretis's clarification of queer issues as they relate to a discussion of lesbian identity, and her rereading of Freud via a discussion of heterosexist feminist readings of psychoanalysis which contain problematic ideas about lesbianism, makes de Lauretis's book a significant intervention into both Freudian theory and theories of lesbian identity. Elizabeth Grosz has described this book as 'the culmination and point of intersection of the feminist fascination with psychoanalytic theory which emerged twenty years ago, and the more recent political eruption of queer politics in the 1990s'.[70]

In *The Practice of Love* de Lauretis discusses lesbianism via Freudian psychoanalysis, Foucauldian discourse theory and the semiotics of Peirce.[71] It is within this framework that she argues how lesbian desires are possible sites of agency for the female body:

> The translation of public fantasy into private fantasy in sexuality, like the join of individual experience and social meanings in identity ... rests on a process of mediation akin to what Peirce called habit, the term by which (in *Alice Doesn't*) I sought to identify the semiotic juncture of inner and outer worlds. In order to describe the process by which the social subject is produced as a sexual subject and a subjectivity, I consider sexuality as a particular instance of semiosis, the more general process joining subjectivity to social signification and material reality. Thus Peirce's notions of interpretant and habit-change may serve to articulate Freud's privatized view of the internal world of the psyche with Foucault's eminently social view of sexuality, by providing an account of the manner in which the implantation of sexuality as perversion actually occurs in one subject, one body-ego.[72]

De Lauretis's multi-directional approach is, indeed, perhaps the best way to conduct a rereading of Freudian psychoanalysis in relation to lesbianism; however, we should also consider whether such a rereading is actually necessary. Her take on Freud enables a discussion of lesbian sexuality as something which is constructed internally in an individual, but which denies the privileging role of the phallus in lesbian sexuality. In relation to the threat of the loss of the phallus via castration in Freudian theory, de Lauretis symbolically replaces the phallus with the female body. It is this symbolic exchange that I regard as the most radical message in this book, and an argument which I will examine in more depth in a moment. However, I would first like to discuss how de Lauretis uses the terms 'sexuality' and 'identity' in relation to subjectivity. In the quote above she suggests that sexuality is an instance of semiosis, and part of a more general process which joins 'subjectivity to social signification and material reality'. She describes identity as a different instance of semiosis which constructs subjectivity through joining 'individual experience' to 'social meanings'. She sees sexuality and identity, then, as instances of semiosis which construct subjectivity by imposing different structures on the transitions between 'inner and outer worlds' – between psychic and material experiences.

In my analysis of lesbian identity and culture, however, I find it difficult to think about the distinction between inner and outer worlds, about 'the sexual drive' or 'the psyche' apart from the ways in which *ideas* about the sexual drive or the psyche are employed by individuals to produce social meanings. This is not to say that there are no drives, for example; rather, it is to insist that sexual drives and the experience of sexual drives, which mark sexualities in particular ways, are mediated through various discourses which describe and constitute them. Psychoanalysis is certainly one (among many) of these discourses, but I want to argue that it has an interconnected relationship with other specific sites of lesbian cultural practice, such as watching lesbian films, reading lesbian publications, attending Pride marches, setting up lesbian rights campaigns, reading and writing lesbian theory, and, in general, living from day to day as a lesbian and as part of lesbian culture. The psyche also exists through other such practices of cultural mediation.

One area of de Lauretis's book which is particularly relevant to my study of lesbian cultural practices is her discussion of lesbian fetishism (see my analysis in Chapter Four). De Lauretis's theory of fetishism relies on the castration complex and the notion of 'disavowal'. To clarify what de Lauretis means by 'disavowal' here, it is important to outline her main challenge to Freud, and how both Freud and de Lauretis centralize the castration complex.

Freud's castration complex is central to the rest of his theory. In Freudian theory lesbian desire is figured in terms of the 'masculinity complex', which is the result of an unresolved Oedipus complex in the lesbian as a girl – a kind of 'faulty' development. In this 'faulty' scenario, rather than reluctantly accepting her own lack of the phallus and desiring those who 'have' it – men – the girl disavows her own castrated condition and retains a masculine and active identity. However, it must be remembered that Freud admitted his theory of the Oedipus complex in girls was poor: 'in general our insight into these developmental processes in girls is unsatisfactory, incomplete and vague'.[73]

De Lauretis's aim, however, is to move beyond the masculinity complex and to understand lesbian sexuality as perversity in terms of disavowal rather than repression. To this end, de Lauretis replaces Freud's fetish object of body *part* with the *entire* female body, arguing that it is not the absence of a penis on her own body that the *girl* disavows but, rather, the absence of another (her mother's, or even her own) woman's body that the *woman* disavows, and must displace onto a fetish substitute. This confusing manoeuvre is the most significant of the book: de Lauretis is suggesting that the threat of sexual repression lesbians are subject to may be turned around into a constitutive space of lesbian subjectivity through the notion of perversion. Here, she articulates the interrelationship of subversive agency with perversion which characterizes queer theory. However, unlike Dollimore and Sedgwick, she bestows agency on the lesbian subject and renounces the privilege accorded to male sexuality in psychoanalytic theory's symbolization of the phallus in the castration narrative.

To exemplify her argument de Lauretis reinscribes the notion of castration with a reference to the character of Stephen Gordon in Radclyffe Hall's *The Well of Loneliness*.[74] She chooses a passage from this text to analyse precisely because: 'it inscribes a fantasy of the female body that works against the grain of the novel's explicit message'.[75] This extract describes Stephen touching her own masculine body, which she hates, in a mirror. De Lauretis argues: 'It is the paternal phallus, inscribed in her very body ... that imposes the taboo which renders the female body' (of her mother, other women's or her own) 'forever inaccessible to Stephen', and thus signifies her 'dispossession' and 'castration'.[76]

In de Lauretis's theory fetishism, which Freud argued was not present in women, is present because the woman's body acts as, or rather instead of, the phallus in this castration scenario. She notes that what the lesbian desires is the female body or something related to it: for example, dress codes, mannerisms and other cultural signifiers of lesbian identity. In this respect de Lauretis's view of lesbian desire centres on the cultural signifiers that characterize lesbian subculture, avoiding a traditional psychoanalytic model that views female sexual desire as active only in relation to the masculinity complex and penis-envy. Notably, de Lauretis reworks Lacan's theory of the (symbolic) phallus in order to renegotiate the terms through which lesbians are 'subjected' to the symbolic law, suggesting that they are, perversely, subjects *in spite of* this law.

De Lauretis's theory demonstrates a radical approach to the 'lesbian question'. Successfully placing lesbianism at the centre of a queer theory, she thus undercuts the male-specific theories of Sedgwick and Dollimore. However, my concern with de Lauretis's book is over how seriously she takes Freudian theory in the first instance. Her extrapolation of Freud here is certainly interesting, if binaristic, but is it wise to use Freudian theory as a foundation upon which to build a theory of lesbian identity that places so much importance on subcultural practices? De Lauretis's understanding of sexuality in relation to identity is based on the premise of an inner psychic world, to which sexual desires and sexual fantasies belong, and an outer world, which is social experience or material reality. In Chapter Five I will suggest that the fantasies and desires of lesbian fans for their lesbian idols are constructed through cultural mediation – where meanings are made in relation to representation, knowledges about lesbian identity, the discourses of stardom and romance, and via a notion of 'the gaze', and not through a psychic field of pleasure, desire and fantasy.

Elizabeth Grosz, in a review of de Lauretis's *The Practice of Love*, maintains that de Lauretis's thesis poses important questions about whether theorizing lesbian desire should involve the addition of lesbians into the psychoanalytic scenario. Grosz rightly questions whether psychoanalysis is at all useful in the analysis of lesbian desire, poignantly asking: 'Does de Lauretis function to provide a political rationale and credibility for psychoanalysis as it lies dying?'[77]

Grosz maintains that for de Lauretis to rework lesbian desire under the auspices of the masculinity complex is inadequate because it subsumes women under a phallic regime. However, if we take de Lauretis's argument as queer theory, the way she perverts the masculinity complex in Freudian theory appears pivotal in her argument for lesbian subjectivity. It is certainly perverse to rework the part of psychoanalysis that most condemns lesbian activity so that it inadvertently produces the possibility for seeing either *masculine or feminine* lesbians as active subjects.

Grosz also wonders about the phallic status of fetishism. Her concern is that if lesbian theorists take up the idea of the fetish, it will be accompanied by a subsequent phallocentric framework: 'if the fetish is just as implicated in masculinity as the phallus then a theory which displaces the masculinity complex with fetishism does not necessarily leave lesbianism any better off'.[78]

The question of whether or not to work with the idea of fetishism in lesbian theory is certainly a significant problem when it comes to theorizing lesbian identity, and particularly lesbian desire. In Chapter Four I will argue that readings of the lesbian idols kd and Martina are structured by fetishism, in the sense that fetishism is the route by which lesbianism is sometimes reproduced in the dominant heterosexual media. In this chapter I conduct an analysis of how lesbian fetishism – or, perhaps more correctly, the fetishization of the lesbian in contemporary western culture – provides an important reference point for understanding the constitution of lesbian identity in terms of signification and the production of subcultural meanings. Rather than grounding my analysis in psychoanalytic theory, I consider the ways in which lesbians construct identity and culture in relation to, and in resistance to, attempts within heterosexual culture to fetishize 'the lesbian' as an object for masculine heterosexual desire and consumption.

Elizabeth Grosz and Lesbian Desire

In 'Refiguring Lesbian Desire' Elizabeth Grosz offers a way of discussing lesbian desire without the constraints of psychoanalytic theory; she also departs from the analyses of identity that have structured the theories of Butler, de Lauretis and Fuss:

> I don't want to discuss lesbian identity or desire in terms of a psychical depth or interiority, or in terms of a genesis, development or process of constitution, history or etiology. I am much less interested in where lesbian desire comes from, how it emerges, and the ways in which it develops than in where it is going to, its possibilities, its open-ended future. I am interested in how to embrace this openness, to welcome unknown readings, new claims, provocative analyses – to make things

happen, to move fixed positions, to transform our everyday expectations and our habitual conceptual schemas.[79]

To dispense with a psychoanalytic notion of desire and lack, and so avoid the problem of the exclusion of women from the psychoanalytic theory of desire, Grosz draws on the writing of Deleuze and Guatarri. She uses the Deleuzian notion of 'becoming'[80] to produce a new understanding of lesbian desire:

> Becoming lesbian, if I can put it this way, is no longer or not simply a question of being lesbian, of identifying with that being known as lesbian, of residing in a position or identity. The question is not am I – or are you – a lesbian but, rather, what kinds of lesbian connections, what kinds of lesbian-machine, we invest our time, energies, and bodies in, what kinds of sexuality we invest ourselves in, with what kinds of bodies, with what bodies of our own, and with what effects? What is it that together, in parts and bits and interconnections, we can make that is new, that is exploratory, that opens up further spaces, induces further intensities, speeds up, enervates, and proliferates production (production of the body, production of the world)?[81]

Grosz's understanding of lesbianism here is similar to the definition of lesbian culture that I sketched out in Chapter One. In my view, the focus she places on the future, and on the transformation of the body and the world through production, is important, as it opens up new possibilities for talking about the transformative potential of lesbian cultural and social production and identity formation. This is how I attempt to analyse lesbian cultural practice in the context of lesbian stardom and fandom in subsequent chapters of this book.

Conclusion

In this chapter I have illustrated some of the tensions that exist in the writings on lesbian identity, culture and desire of theorists from a wide range of academic disciplines. In the subsequent chapters of this book I will suggest, contrary to the queer theories of Dollimore and Sedgwick that prioritize signs of male homosexuality, that lesbian identity is being produced, and reproduced, in relation to an increasing proliferation of the cultural signs *of* lesbian identity.

The rise to fame of kd lang and Martina Navratilova as lesbian *stars* in the mainstream media sanctions lesbianism as a social identity in a way that would have been impossible to imagine ten years ago. I would suggest that this phenomenon not only challenges the invisibility of lesbianism but also questions conventional understandings of sexual and gender difference, and thus troubles the very core of heterosexual systems of knowledge about masculinity and femininity, and even the very categories of man and woman and an understanding of 'sex'.

Queer theories, in my view, do not allow us to understand these challenges to heterosexuality, as such theories imply that male homosexuality is more subversive of heterosexual knowledge systems than structures of lesbian identification, a conviction that is characteristic of queer politics at a wider level, where the fight against homophobia is conducted by mainly white gay men. Hence, whilst white gay men may be subordinated on the grounds of sexuality, and rightly protest at such oppression, theorists such as Dollimore and Sedgwick offer no critique of the system of differences that procures such an oppression. By contrast, they merely select the issue of male homosexuality within the structure of western society as a whole, arguing that, in fact, all identifications are driven either by male homosexual desire or its repression. Such analyses, then, pivoting as they do on psychoanalytic logic, regard lesbian identifications as 'by the way' identifications which have no destabilizing effect on a heterosexist society.

So, as I noted earlier in this chapter, Judith Butler, in *Bodies that Matter*, suggests that the word 'queer' derives its power through 'the repeated invocation by which it has become linked to accusation, pathologization, insult'.[82] However, she also warns of the inherent risk which attends every use of identity categories such as 'queer' – just as the word derives power from the reappropriation of a previous negative usage, it is also impossible to secure its use in the future. In other words, 'queer' may hold radical potential for certain groups of individuals who alter its meaning according to their own specific requirements. Dollimore and Sedgwick are two such examples in the academic context.

In my view Butler's radical work has been taken up by other theorists who interject the word 'queer' into their arguments with the effect of making its meaning simple and unproblematic, and are thus producing a 'queer theory' which stretches over much wider theoretical terrain than the theories of Dollimore and Sedgwick. The popularity of 'queer theory' in academia, and the apparent inability to recognize crucial differences between male-oriented queer theory and the kind of analysis that Butler, de Lauretis and Grosz have offered, has forestalled a much-needed discussion about the problems inherent in the notion of queer and the theoretical routes through which it has developed.

In this book, I have tracked back to Butler's *Gender Trouble* in order to understand challenges to heterosexual systems of sexual and gender difference produced through lesbian cultural practices. As my analysis concentrates on the relationship between representation and identity formation through modes of consumption, I have also, to some extent, worked with a notion of signification. The way I employ semiotics, here, which is influenced by de Lauretis's work in *Technologies of Gender*, enables the theorization of identity in relation to the production of meaning in contextualized social and cultural contexts. Such concerns are central to Butler's, de Lauretis's and Grosz's feminist theories of lesbian sexuality – concerns which, I would argue, have been permanently under siege by attempts to jump on a queer bandwagon, for the sake of novelty, perhaps, but certainly publication.

Notes

1. See Laura Cottingham, *Lesbians Are So Chic ... that We're Not Really Lesbians at All* (London and New York: Cassell, 1996).

2. Judith Butler, *Gender Trouble: Feminism and the Subversion of Identity* (London and New York: Routledge, 1990); 'Imitation and Gender Insubordination' in Diana Fuss (ed.), *Inside/Out: Lesbian Theories, Gay Theories* (London and New York: Routledge, 1991), pp. 13–31; *Bodies that Matter: On the Discursive Limits of 'Sex'* (London and New York: Routledge, 1993).

3. Teresa de Lauretis, *Technologies of Gender: Essays on Theory, Film and Fiction* (London: Macmillan, 1987); *The Practice of Love: Lesbian Sexuality and Perverse Desire* (Bloomington and Indianapolis: Indiana University Press, 1994).

4. Elisabeth Grosz, 'Refiguring Lesbian Desire' in Laura Doan (ed.), *The Lesbian Postmodern* (New York: Columbia University Press, 1994), pp. 67–84; 'The Labours of Love, Analysing Perverse Desire: An Interrogation of Teresa de Lauretis's *The Practice of Love*', *Differences*, Vol. 6, nos 2 and 3, Summer-Autumn 1994, pp. 274–95.

5. Butler, 'Imitation and Gender Insubordination', p. 14.

6. Eve Sedgwick, *Epistemology of the Closet* (Berkeley, Los Angeles: University of California Press, 1990); 'Queer Performativity: Henry James's *The Art of the Novel*', *GLQ*, Vol. 1 Pt 1, Spring 1993.

7. Jonathan Dollimore, *Sexual Dissidence: Augustine to Wilde,*

Freud to Foucault (Oxford: Oxford University Press, 1991); 'The Cultural Politics of Perversion: Augustine, Shakespeare, Freud, Foucault' in Joe Bristow (ed.), *Sexual Sameness* (London and New York: Routledge, 1992), pp. 9–25.

8. *Ibid.*

9. Michel Foucault's *The History of Sexuality: An Introduction* (London: Peregrine, 1984) has been productively used by feminist and lesbian theorists – particularly Judith Butler – because he puts forward a convincing and interesting analysis of contemporary society. However, the absence of lesbians from his study of sexuality does mark his theory as highly problematic. Further, his analysis of discourse, particularly in this, his most often quoted book, does sometimes tend to assert that power is endemic to society, and, thus, his notion of the social is at times reductionist.

10. Dollimore, 'The Cultural Politics of Perversion', p. 12.

11. *Ibid.*, emphasis in original.

12. *Ibid.*, p. 14, emphasis in original.

13. *Ibid.*, emphasis in original.

14. Alexander Doty, *Making Things Perfectly Queer: Interpreting Mass Culture* (Minneapolis: University of Minnesota Press, 1993), p. 16.

15. Dollimore, *Sexual Dissidence*, p. 228.

16. For a discussion of how this is possible, see Diana Fuss, *Essentially Speaking: Feminism, Nature and Difference* (London and New York: Routledge, 1989).

17. *Ibid.*

18. Eve Sedgwick, *Epistemology of the Closet* p. 1.

19. Like Dollimore, Sedgwick does not acknowledge that Foucault's theory of sexuality omits a study of lesbianism.

20. Sedgwick, *Epistemology of the Closet*, p. 1.

21. Sedgwick, *Epistemology of the Closet*, p. 11.

22. *Ibid.*

23. Herman Melville, *Billy Budd* (Aerie Books, 1988, first published in 1924).

24. Sedgwick, *Epistemology of the Closet*, p. 96.

25. Adrienne Rich, 'Compulsory Heterosexuality and Lesbian Existence', *Signs*, Vol. 5 No. 4, Summer 1980, pp. 631–60.

26. For an analysis of the benefits of Rich's article see Deborah Cameron, 'Old Het?', *Trouble and Strife*, No. 24, Summer 1992, pp. 41–5.

27. Sedgwick, 'Queer Performativity'. Emphasis in original.

28. *Ibid.*, p. 4.

29. Mary McIntosh, 'Queer Theory and the War of the Sexes' in Joe Bristow and Angela R. Wilson (eds), *Activating Theory: Lesbian, Gay, Bisexual Politics* (London: Lawrence and Wishart, 1993), pp. 30–52.

30. *Ibid.*, p. 47.

31. Cherry Smyth, *Lesbians Talk Queer Notions* (London: Scarlet Press, 1992).

32. *Ibid.*, p. 11.

33. 'Abjection' is a notion that Judith Butler takes up in *Bodies that Matter*.

34. Helen (charles), 'Queer Nigger: Theorizing "White" Activism' in Bristow and Wilson (eds), *Activating Theory*, pp. 97–106.

35. McIntosh, 'Queer Theory', p. 31.

36. Butler, *Bodies that Matter*, p. 226.

37. The way that individuals are 'hailed' or interpellated in terms of their social position is what Louis Althusser suggests in 'Ideology and Ideological State Apparatuses (Notes Towards an Investigation) (January–April 1969)' in *Lenin and*

Philosophy and Other Essays, translated from the French by Ben Brewster, (London: NLB, 1971), pp. 121–73.

38. For an example of post-colonial theory see Donna Haraway, 'The Promises of Monsters: A Regenerative Politics for Inappropriate/d Others' in Lawrence Grossberg (ed.), *Cultural Studies* (London and New York: Routledge, 1992), pp. 295–337; and Homi K. Bhabha, *The Location of Culture* (London and New York: Routledge, 1994).

39. Butler, *Gender Trouble*; 'Imitation and Gender Insubordination'; *Bodies that Matter.*

40. De Lauretis, *Technologies of Gender; The Practice of Love.*

41. Grosz, 'Refiguring Lesbian Desire'; 'The Labours of Love'.

42. Butler, 'Imitation and Gender Insubordination', pp. 13–14.

43. In *Heavenly Bodies: Film Stars and Society* (London: BFI/Macmillan, 1992), Richard Dyer stresses how the consumption of Judy Garland is important to gay identifications.

44. Butler, 'Imitation and Gender Insubordination', p. 14.

45. De Lauretis, *Technologies of Gender*, p. 5.

46. *Ibid.*

47. *Ibid.*, p. 25. De Lauretis's idea of another perspective – or a view from 'elsewhere' – is similar to the post-colonial theories put forward by Haraway in 'The Promises of Monsters' and Bhabha in *The Location of Culture.*

48. *Ibid.*

49. For a similar analysis of lesbian identity in relation to current theoretical fields see Diana Fuss, *Essentially Speaking.*

50. Butler, *Gender Trouble*, p. x.

51. *Ibid.*, p. 7.

52. *Ibid.*, pp. 24–5.

53. *Ibid.*, p. 20.

54. Sigmund Freud, quoted in Butler, *ibid.*, p. 60.

55. *Ibid.*, p. 60.

56. *Ibid.*, pp. 60–1, emphasis in original.

57. *Ibid.*, p. 64.

58. *Ibid.*, pp. 64–5.

59. For a comprehensive analysis of both Freudian and Lacanian theory see Juliet Mitchel and Jacqueline Rose (eds), *Feminine Sexuality: Jaques Lacan and the École Freudienne* (London: Macmillan Press, 1985).

60. Butler, *Gender Trouble*, p. 53.

61. *Ibid.*, p. 55.

62. *Ibid.*, p. 122, emphasis in original.

63. *Ibid.*, p. 137, emphasis in original.

64. *Ibid.*, p. 139.

65. *Ibid.*, p. 93.

66. Butler, *Bodies that Matter*, p. 2.

67. *Ibid.*, p. 3.

68. *Ibid.*, p. 7.

69. See Mitchel and Rose, *Feminine Sexuality.*

70. Grosz, 'The Labours of Love', p. 274.

71. For analyses of semiotics see Terence Hawkes, *Structuralism and Semiotics* (London and New York: Routledge, 1989); Ferdinand de Saussure, *Course in General Linguistics* (London: Duckworth, 1990); Claude Levi-Strauss, *The Raw and the Cooked: Introduction to a Science of Mythology* (London: Penguin, 1992); Roland Barthes, *Mythologies* (New York: Noonday Press, 1992); Rosalind Coward and John Ellis, *Language and Materialism: Developments in Semiology and the Theory of the Subject* (London and New York: Routledge, 1993).

72. De Lauretis, *The Practice of Love*, p. xix.

73. Sigmund Freud, 'The Dissolution of the Oedipus Complex' in *On Sexuality* (London: Pelican Books,

1977, first published in 1924), pp. 314–22.

74. Radclyffe Hall, *The Well of Loneliness* (London: Virago, 1984, first published by Jonathan Cape in 1928).

75. De Lauretis, *The Practice of Love*, p. 209.

76. *Ibid.*, p. 212.

77. Grosz, 'The Labours of Love', p. 278.

78. *Ibid.*, p. 290.

79. Grosz, 'Refiguring Lesbian Desire', pp. 68–9.

80. *Ibid.*, p. 80.

81. *Ibid.*, p. 81.

82. Butler, *Bodies that Matter*, p. 226.

3

Lesbian Idols, Lesbian Images

Introduction

Photographic images are central to any star/fan relationship, and so are the possibilities that the pin-up provides for 'starlust'. Photographic images of kd and Martina, then, are important cultural items that may help us to understand how fan consumption practices interweave both with practices of identification and with processes of subcultural resistance to dominant media images.

In this chapter I will analyse specific images of kd and Martina, to assess how representations of these stars may be consumed by audiences, and how specific meanings of gender, sex, race and ethnicity may be produced in this context of lesbian idolization. I will adhere to the premise that the 'meaning' of a text is produced in the relations of production, circulation and consumption of that text, and in relation to the dominations and subordinations which provide the social context for these processes. It follows, then, that when these relationships in a society shift, meanings also have the potential to change. Hence, I will examine several representations of kd and Martina and analyse whether they may be read in ways which challenge dominant ideas about sex, gender, race and ethnicity.

In the highly technological, consumer-oriented commodity culture of the late twentieth century the representation of identities through cultural products such as magazines, films and advertisements has become commonplace. Thus, with the rapid succession of different fashions and lifestyles, the meanings of images produced within the mainstream media are open to question much more frequently than they were twenty, or even ten, years ago.

The idea that identities may be constructed through the relationship between representational practices and readings of such practices is central to the arguments I put forward in this chapter. Often, heterosexual identities are represented as ideal in the context of stardom, but how are lesbian identities being represented, and consumed, through the stardom of kd and Martina? Does this form of representation merely reproduce negative ideas about lesbians as 'deviants' and 'perverts', or does it offer possibilities for meaning-making which deconstruct this idea? Ultimately, we need to ask how are kd and Martina constructed as *ideal* through modes of representation used in media stardom?

Significantly, even though, as I have suggested, lesbian identity and culture have developed through existing historical and social continuums, there is a sense in which the consumer of a photograph of Martina does not pre-exist the reading of the photograph as a 'lesbian reader', any more than Martina, say, pre-exists the photograph as a 'lesbian star'. The construction of both Martina as a lesbian star and the consumer of a photograph of Martina as a lesbian reader takes place in a process within which photographic discourse has a formalizing role in the production of identity. Thus lesbian identity is both produced and *re*produced in these contexts of consumption. This is not to say, however, that no 'real' lesbian truly exists, but rather to point out that representation is key to understanding the very concept of identity in the modern era.

In her article 'Imitation and Gender Insubordination'[1] Judith Butler clarifies this point when she suggests that the notion of lesbian identity is constituted through 'repetition', and that this repetition may highlight how identities might *appear* unified. Although at one level this kind of analysis does not explain how something can be repeated if nothing precedes it; at another level, if we think about lesbian culture and identity as being continually reproduced, and recognize that representation plays a key role in this reproduction, it is possible to understand how continuums of meaning can come into play. Butler argues:

> The prospect of *being* anything, even for pay, has always produced in me a certain anxiety, for 'to be' gay, 'to be' lesbian seems to be more than a simple injunction to become who or what I already am. And in no way does it settle the anxiety for me to say that this is 'part' of what I am. To write or speak *as a lesbian* appears a paradoxical appearance of this 'I', one which feels neither true nor false. For it is a production, usually in response to a request, to come out or write in the name of an identity which, once produced, sometimes functions as a politically efficacious phantasm.[2]

I would suggest, then, that the act of reading a particular text as a representation of a lesbian star is also an act of repetition, in Butler's meaning, through which a lesbian identity is constructed. However, I want to argue that we know this is a repetition of lesbian identity because of the historical and social aspects which have intersected to produce 'the lesbian' both as a category and as a 'lived out' identity.

One way that heterosexual identity is traditionally conventionalized in western society is through the discourse of stardom and the repetition of heterosexual identities involved in this discourse. I want to ask whether lesbian identity is also being conventionalized in this context of star representation. This is a radical suggestion, because lesbian identity is traditionally seen as deviant or unnatural in a homophobic western society.

The photographic images of Martina and kd are important to my analysis because they often appear in *mainstream* magazines and news-papers. (By 'mainstream' representation I mean representation through the dominant modes of production in contemporary society, through which dominant ideas about ideal identities such as heterosexuality, whiteness and gender conformity become cemented.) Therefore, kd and Martina's status as lesbian idols is constructed through *dominant* modes of cultural production, and not only through the usual 'alternative' methods of production whereby lesbian identities have historically been reproduced.

One example of such alternative lesbian cultural production is the 'lesbian art photography' of Della Grace. This kind of work is shown in small independent galleries and reproduced in subcultural or left-wing magazines, and attracts a predominantly lesbian audience. This work is certainly valuable because of the importance of visibility for subordinated identities; however, my analysis emphasizes the effect that practices of consumption, rather than production, have on the meanings of visual cultural reproduction. It then becomes possible to understand how resistance to oppression may take place through specific readings by specific types of consumers, of texts produced in the mainstream.

In order to argue that lesbian identity is idealized and, thus, conventionalized in the context of the stardom of kd and Martina, I will examine how photographs of these lesbian idols, taken when they were struggling to establish their careers and were relatively unknown, are later re-presented in newspaper and magazine articles about their rise to fame, effectively reconstructing them as 'real' people and 'real' lesbians for consumption by an audience. In this way paradoxically, the low-status identity of lesbianism has been authenticated, an authentication which also allows lesbian fans to identify with their idols.

Using specific photographs of Martina and kd taken throughout their careers, I will illustrate how the production of ideal identities takes place in popular culture, subsequently exploring the tension between an authentication of lesbian identity produced in the context of lesbian stardom and the possibilities for disrupting heterosexist identity regimes through the representation of a traditionally deviant lesbian identity through the star discourse.

Ordinary People

One of the central factors that accounts for the rise to fame of Martina and kd is the shift that occurred in their careers, transforming them from 'ordinary people' into stars. Although this shift is not unusual in terms of the heterosexual star process, it is the lesbian identification with these stars which produces their status as lesbian idols.

In *Heavenly Bodies*, Richard Dyer discusses the way in which gay men identify with Judy Garland. He argues that 'ordinariness' has a great deal to do with this identification, suggesting that Garland's early MGM image as the ordinary heterosexual girl next door contrasted with her later image when her unhappy life became more public. Dyer contends that these later MGM performances reflected the pathos in her private life, and goes on to maintain that gay men identified with her because, like Garland, most gay men follow a similar path from ordinary to 'not-ordinary':

> One is not brought up gay; on the contrary, everything in the culture seems to work against it. Had Garland remained an image of ordinary normality, like June Allyson or Deanna Durbin (who proved her normality by leaving Hollywood and settling down, happily married), she would not have been so available as a gay icon. It was the fact, as became clear after 1950, that she was not after all the ordinary girl she appeared to be that suggested a relationship to ordinariness homologous with that of gay identity. To turn out not-ordinary after being saturated with the values of ordinariness structures Garland's career and the standard gay biography alike.[3]

Although there are differences between the scenario of Judy Garland as a gay icon and kd or Martina as lesbian icons (kd and Martina have the same sexuality as their lesbian fans, thus making them instantly available as lesbian icons), it is clear that the star as 'ordinary' and then 'not-ordinary' is significant in terms of the availability of that star to a gay or lesbian audience, an availability that is clearly grounded in shared experience and recognition.

The move from 'ordinary person' to star necessarily involves the idea that a person has struggled to achieve fame. This idea of struggle is also central to the heterosexual construction of identity through stardom, but it carries a different meaning when understood in the context of lesbian stardom. This element of struggle makes kd and Martina appealing for lesbian audiences because it can be read as analogous to the struggle involved in achieving and maintaining a lesbian identity.

In retrospective articles and features about the careers of stars in magazines and newspapers, outdated photographs charting their early careers are often re-presented to contrast the 'now famous' star with the 'real' person before their success. In the face of the mass cultural replication of a star image, which may at times appear depthless or superficial, this technique enables the viewer to identify with their idol as a 'real' person, thus authenticating the identity that the star represents.

Rags to Riches

Having discovered Patsy Cline in 1982, kd lang developed an interest in country and western music, adopting its dress codes quite early in her career, before she achieved widespread popular success. Initially she had shown a taste for creating music that did not comply with conventional codes or genres. This was also reflected in a taste for 'alternative' dress codes and lifestyle.

In her biography of kd lang, Victoria Starr describes how kd 'got involved with a group of local bohemians' when she lived in Canada in the late 1970s.[4] She was also described by friends, Starr notes, as '"a real beatnik type"'[5] because she cut her own hair, was a vegetarian and made 'alternative' music at Red Deer college. Starr suggests that the mixture of kd's 'spiky, home-made hair cuts' and the way she wore outfits which were 'a hodge podge of country kitsch, with long, full skirts, torn stockings and blouses with rhinestone buttons' made her look 'a bit like a cowboy in drag'.[6]

One particular photograph[7] published in Starr's biography recalls kd's early career in the early 1980s. In this image kd's 'otherness' is represented through her difference from the appearance of more conventional female figures within the country music genre, such as Dolly Parton. Significantly, this otherness occurs in relation to gender. Parton's long blonde hair, her abundant use of make-up and her highly feminized dresses and skirts, which were ornamented with tassels and sequins and cut to enhance the shape of her overwhelming bosom, contrast sharply with the indicators of 'boyishness' in this, and indeed many other, images of kd. Here, kd has short hair and wears a country-style frock (decorated with plastic cowboy figures) which does nothing to enhance the extremities of her figure. Wearing a pair of glasses reminiscent of those worn by Patsy Cline, she completes the ensemble with cut-down cowboy boots.

All these factors, which cast kd as 'other' from the conventional image of femininity within the country music genre, make it easy for lesbian identification to take place, as lesbian identity has often encompassed the rejection of traditionally feminine codes.[8] This image of the 'crazy kid', or 'mad teenager' signifies the struggle that kd experienced in her early career. More recent appearances in mainstream magazines such as *Vanity Fair* have pictured her in much more stylish poses, hair cuts and clothes.

Although in star discourse in general idols are often constructed within the 'rags to riches' framework, this idea is particularly relevant in relation to the country music genre. Stuart Ewen, in a book dealing with the representation of style in western culture, discusses the country singing star in a chapter on stardom. He explains the relation of the Nashville music scene to the process of stardom and illustrates how the country and western music genre encourages 'ordinary people' to become household names:

> If anything, the ongoing message of the celebrisystem is that through its channels the 'underlying population' can achieve the status of 'those at the top'. In Nashville, Tennessee's music district, where the names and faces of country and western stars are emblazoned in a crazy-quilt tribute to upward mobility, one also finds several small-scale recording studios which are 'open to the public'.[9]

Ewen goes on to point out the way in which identification is facilitated by the transformation of the 'ordinary person' into a star:

Celebrities, though they shine above us, are also – many of them – very much like us and identification is easy. The whole story of their success is that they come from 'the mass'. They were once unknown. In a society where conditions of anonymity fertilize the desire 'to be somebody', the *dream of identity*, the *dream of wholeness*, is intimately woven together with the desire to be known; to be visible; to be documented, for all to see.[10]

There is a striking similarity here between stardom in the way Ewen describes it, and lesbian identity. A lesbian who has not 'come out' and feels oppressed or isolated from other lesbians may desire to take on a visible lesbian identity in order to feel 'whole'. A similar scenario surrounds the unknown singer or actor, whose desire to be known, and therefore visible, is acute, and for them holds the key to a 'whole' identity. Therefore it seems that a lesbian identification with kd has as much to do with the *process* of stardom and kd's underlying 'ordinariness' as with the fact that she is now a famous 'out' lesbian.

The following extracts from the letters I received highlight just how important are the 'ordinary lives' of lesbian idols to their lesbian fans:

These two women share similar aspects in their lives. Both have had parents who divorced. Likewise both are out lesbians. They have strong points of view on varying aspects of life, and neither come from rich backgrounds as such. Both are emotionally sensitive and have a good sense of humour. All these points I believe have to a certain degree given them a deep driving determination to get to the top, to overcome the hardships and negative aspects of life and become perfectionists.

(Dorothy, a kd and Martina fan)

I feel I have more in common with kd than Annie [Lennox] and that's definitely due in part to her being a lesbian, but also to the fact she seems more down to earth. Annie always seemed a bit aloof and quite definitely a 'star' in interviews, whereas kd seems much more human and real. She played sport when she was young and rode around town playing at Starsky and Hutch (if the biography is to be believed) which are all the things I did.

(June, a kd fan)

Here, being a lesbian, playing 'tomboyish' childhood games, overcoming family traumas and having little money all signify the lesbian star's authenticity to their lesbian fans. Again, the fans make a strong link between authenticity and lesbianism: the 'rags to riches' idea, then, is central to both the construction of stars and a lesbian identity.

East to West
Sport, like Nashville, also offers the possibility of stardom for 'ordinary people'. Nashville, however, is primarily concerned with producing *stars*. Sport, on the other hand, has traditionally been a place where talented competitors achieve fame within the sporting arena, but, on the whole, do not become internationally renowned media stars or household names and images. However, along with athletics, basketball and football, tennis is one area of sport where this is changing.

The international tennis circuit has invested heavily in the commodification strategies of contemporary consumer culture. Sports advertisers use the spaces on players' hats, shirts, skirts and shorts to display their goods. The growth of the leisure industry has ensured the mass appeal of playing tennis, which is sold to the public as a particularly stylish activity. Players patent rackets, sportswear and even their own brands of designer underwear: men's singles players such as Bjorn Borg and André Agassi have brought out their own range of boxer shorts. Within this expanding orgy of commodification, successful tennis players have achieved a celebrity-like position as media stars.

Central to this phenomenon is the notion of style. At the 1995 Wimbledon championship Agassi's outfit included a white bandanna, worn to cover his crew-cut hairstyle, dangling gold earrings and long-legged designer shorts. The tennis commentators referred to this as the 'pirate look' (indeed, his well-played shots were on occasion followed by shouts of 'Aarh, Jim lad' from his supporters). Significantly, this image could have fitted equally as well in a lifestyle magazine as in the sports section of a newspaper.

It is within this context of the rise to media stardom of tennis players that we must understand Martina's status as a lesbian idol. However, the ways in which audiences may identify with Agassi are vastly different from the ways in which they may identify with Martina. Agassi's star appeal resides in the prominence accorded to his 'designer' fashion style, an increased emphasis on style that represents a shift in western culture, as Ewen points out:

> With the shifting conception of value, from concrete tangibility to the mobile immateriality of the abstract, the aesthetic dimension of style has shifted as well. If more traditional incarnations paid tribute to the weighty, and stationary, tangibility of landed wealth, modern style is imprinted with the valued quality of transient unembodied worth.[11]

An important defining feature of Martina's stardom is her appeal to lesbian audiences who identify with her because she is a lesbian; no such demonized sexuality accompanies Agassi's appeal, as he is a heterosexual sex symbol. Rather, he is perhaps idolized more for his exuberant personality and stylistic dress sense than his life experience and social practices.

Thus, particular readings of pictures of 'Martina the sporting celebrity' are more likely to be structured by the idea of struggle involved in the living out of a subordinated lesbian identity. Clearly, this notion of struggle rests on an awareness of her lesbian identity, but it also encompasses the struggle involved in her defection from communist Czechoslovakia. An early photograph of Martina, taken in 1978 when she first won Wimbledon, was published in a retrospective article in the *Guardian* in 1994, which also featured extracts from a biography of the tennis star.[12] The image was included as part of an overview of Martina's early career. The fact that this photograph was printed sixteen years after it was taken illustrates the significance of struggle to the identification with Martina as a lesbian.

Martina is pictured kneeling before the net, which exists as a barrier between her and the camera. Having just played a difficult shot, she watches the ball fly over the net cord, which masks her face, leaving only her eyes visible. The net cord, acting as a symbolic barrier between her and the free-flying ball, is perhaps reminiscent of her struggle to escape from communist rule through gaining US citizenship. The net itself translates into a cage trapping her in the frame of the photograph, whilst the free flight of the ball might also be read as her tennis skill – her ticket out of Czechoslovakia. The masking of her face represents the struggle from young unknown to her identity as an international tennis success.

If this photograph can be read as representative of Martina's struggle for tennis glory and US citizenship, it may also be interpreted in terms of her struggle for lesbian identity. Here is the image of a young lesbian oppressed by heterosexual norms who wishes to free herself from the constraints of living a heterosexual lie. The net that separates us, the audience, from Martina may symbolize the difficulties of finding a lesbian community and the isolation this creates. The division it sets up may also represent the way lesbians are viewed as deviant and on the 'other side' of normative heterosexual behaviour.

Martina's dress in this photograph also confirms our belief that Eastern European fashion lags behind western trends. The USA's cultural domination of Eastern European countries such as Czechoslovakia becomes apparent if we examine the notion of style. Martina's dress with its large garish collars and conspicuous buttons, appears out dated in comparison with the outfits worn by western players at this time. Again this reinforces a western understanding of Eastern European countries as poor, needy and culturally deprived.

This contrast between East and West also references knowledges about lesbian identity. A reading of this kind by lesbian audiences emphasizes Martina's rejection of traditional, but also, importantly, capitalist notions of femininity. Awareness of the high degree of glamour in representations of western female stars contrasts with knowledges about Eastern European women not having access to the kind of commodity culture through which feminine styles or fashions are perpetuated. This is significant in relation to the way in which lesbian identity is often represented in terms of a feminist rejection of patriarchal femininity.[13]

This rejection of conventional codes of femininity by a specific mode of lesbian feminist politics in the 1970s and 1980s is significant in relation to the stereotypical connection often made, for example, by sports commentators, between Eastern European women athletes and masculinity. Gilda Zwerman, in a biography of Martina, maintains that 'Martina brought an unprecedented power and athleticism to women's tennis.'[14] This association of Martina with 'power' in an unprecedented sense for women athletes informs knowledges about both her lesbian and Eastern European identities.[15] This association of Martina with masculinity has often been utilized by dominant heterosexual culture to portray her as deviant and perverted. However, this dominant perception of masculinity must be questioned. Using photographs of Martina I will attempt to highlight redeployments of masculinity in relation to lesbian identity which may alter meanings of the gender classifications of masculinity and femininity.

The authentication of lesbian identities through the concept of a star's inherent 'ordinariness' is just one factor. Other processes render star identities, including lesbian star identities, ideal. Some stars remain ordinary; others, by contrast, never were ordinary. However, often these two processes work together, grounding the star in an identity of ordinariness, whilst simultaneously making the star seem super-human and god-like, beyond reproach. It is this contrast between ordinariness/ authentication and idealization that produces lesbian stardom and the lesbian star/fan relationship.

Within homophobic western culture lesbianism is derided as unnatural through dominating ideological discourses such as biology, psychology, psychiatry, Christian moral rhetoric, criminology, and so on. Therefore, the representation of lesbian identity as both ideal and ordinary (or even *commonplace*) in the context of lesbian stardom is at odds with the wider cultural and social oppression of lesbians. Such a paradoxical construction of the lesbian is indeed radical, and we must question how the representation of lesbian stars in the popular media may disrupt those heterosexist knowledge systems which oppress lesbians more widely. Therefore, in successive sections of this chapter I will examine representations of kd and Martina, in relation to the meanings of gender, sex and ethnicity in these images.

Gender and Difference

One way in which the idealization of identities in the star context takes place is through discourses of *gender*. In conventional star representation, gender difference is represented as inevitable and complementary. In a heterosexual framework of gender, masculinity is seen to reside in a category of 'man', whilst femininity is seen to reside in a category of 'woman'. My aim in this section is to discuss how meanings of gender are redeployed within the context of lesbian stardom. As this involves an exploration of the notions of masculinity and femininity in relation to kd and Martina, I will refer to kd and Martina as 'women'. However, as well as questioning the necessary relationship of masculinity to men and femininity to women, I also want to explore the notion of 'being a woman' – of what it means to 'be' a 'woman'. Even though the idea of being a man or woman would seem to be more socially and culturally embedded than masculinity or femininity, what will hopefully become apparent through my analysis is that both sets of categories are constructed through the same representational strategies.

Courting the Image: 'Martin' or 'Martina'?
The notion of identity is grounded in the sameness/difference binary. Therefore, it would be rash to offer readings of masculinity and femininity in images of Martina and kd without taking this binary model into account. Diana Fuss offers this description of identity:

> Questions of sameness and difference lie at the very heart of traditional metaphysical investigations into the problem of identity. To locate the identity of an object, for example, entails in analytic philosophy determining both whether that object is itself and not a different entity and whether that object remains the same over time.[16]

In the following argument I will establish how Martina's image is constructed in relation to that of Chris Evert through codes of gender.

Two photographs from 1982 (Plates 1 and 2) capture a moment from the battle for the Wimbledon championship which raged between Martina and Chris Evert for many years. The ongoing professional relationship that was established between these two tennis players cemented Martina's masculinity in relation to Chris's femininity. When viewed against most non-sporting women, Chris Evert would appear far from 'feminine'; however, in the sporting context, and especially against Martina, she was constructed by the media not only as a rival to Martina's tennis skill but also to her 'masculine' gender. Evert was specifically constructed in the mainstream press as the ideal female, and feminine, tennis player. She was blonde, wore feminine dresses and her heterosexual romances often hit the headlines.

These images clearly establish the relationship of difference between Martina and Chris, a difference that is reinforced by the acompanying captions. In Plate 2 Evert is pictured 'stretching' sideways, using her double-handed backhand, in a match against Billie Jean King. Chris's double-handed backhand may be read in terms of weakness traditionally associated with conventional femininity, and compares strikingly to Martina's single-handed forehand in Plate 1, and her particularly muscular arms. The caption describes Martina as 'lunging', implying a forwards movement and perhaps also the idea of 'penetration', a quality often associated with a sexualized form of masculinity.

Zwerman examines the difference between Chris Evert and Martina. In a chapter entitled 'The Princess and the Alien' she describes Chris thus:

> She wore pinafore dresses and ribbons in her hair. She was slim and demure. She even played the sport like a lady, hitting even ground strokes from the baseline and seldom displaying emotion during her matches, keeping so cool that some dubbed her the 'ice princess'. At 18, she started dating her counterpart on the men's circuit, the handsome and dashing Jimmy Connors, and the two were presented as tennis's Cinderella and Prince Charming. For corporate America, 'Chrissie' Evert could not have presented a more perfect image: a wholesome, ladylike child champion who, it seemed, rarely even broke a sweat on court.[17]

The language used to describe Chris Evert, emphasized here by Zwerman, supports the view of Chris as more 'feminine' than Martina. That Chris was described as the 'ice princess' may suggest that her feminine character was beyond reproach, even akin to royalty; although, perhaps somewhat conversely, by calling her 'Chrissie', supporters and sports commentators alike made her seem very down-to-earth and even 'ordinary'. This contrast between Evert's ordinariness and Martina's non-ordinariness pertains to normative ideas of gender identity, and also relates to Dyer's analysis of the identification of gay men with Judy Garland – Chris stayed ordinary (heterosexual), but Martina 'came out' as a lesbian and became not-ordinary, in the same way that her lesbian fans were not-ordinary. Thus, in relation to the representation of Chris Evert, remaining ordinary equates to a normative heterosexual feminine identity.

With her 'naturally' blonde hair, in contrast to Martina's bleached hair, Chris was represented to the American and British public as the perfect woman. When she married the respectable English tennis player John Lloyd, who was also blond, they became represented as the perfect trans-Atlantic tennis couple. As Wimbledon was an English tournament, it seemed fitting that America's girl-next-door of tennis should marry an Englishman.

Zwerman also describes Martina's identity in relation to Chris:

> Navratilova, on the other hand, was a big, tough, overweight 'foreigner'. Her Czech origins were still audible in the accent with which she spoke English. Her approach to the sport was

unapologetically athletic. Her arms and legs bulged with muscles. She played tennis aggressively, rushing to the net and taking risks. Her demeanour was anything but ladylike. She expressed everything she was feeling, even during matches. She scowled. She laughed. She stamped her feet. She slapped her hand to her forehead. She yelped for joy. She argued. And she was completely on her own. There was no family to fawn her and there were no boyfriends in sight.[18]

In her description of Martina as 'big', 'tough' and 'overweight', and by suggesting that her muscular legs 'bulged' and that she 'yelped' and 'scowled', we are given the impression that Martina is far less refined than Chris. The language is quite animalistic, and contrasts sharply with Zwerman's description of Evert as 'ladylike'.

Here, signifiers of animal-like behaviour in Martina are alikened to the notion of 'masculinity'. In the context of British 'ladies' tennis, where unfeminine behaviour amongst women players is viewed extremely unfavourably, such an unladylike demeanour is associated with masculinity and, as I argued earlier, Eastern European women. Hence, maintaining Martina's 'otherness' in relation to Chris was critical in perpetuating Evert's feminine image as ideal, and in reinforcing the conventional gender relations which underscore the importance of femininity for western heterosexual women.

This letter, sent to me by a Martina fan, illustrates how Martina is idolized by her fans precisely because she is masculine, in contrast to more conventionally feminine figures; here Miranda contrasts Martina's image with that of *the* icon of British femininity, Princess Diana:

I have fancied Martina since I first started watching women's tennis (quite by chance) when I was 14, and she helped me to decide I was a lesbian. She seemed very strong, slightly more muscular than the fashion was for women. This was 1982, when the media was full of pictures of Princess Diana, who was then very 'frilly', romantic, silly, pretty, plump and blonde. I never liked Princess Di as all my classmates did, because she was portrayed as lovably stupid. At this point in my life I was trying to get away from this label myself – although I always did very well academically, my father was always putting me down about my inability as a 12-year-old to understand his PhD-level maths and physics. At the same time he would 'perve' my already developed body, which got unwanted attention from nearly every man who saw me, it seemed. So I had something of a Princess Di complex. I wanted to get away from this female stereotype, which was beginning to seem like my inevitably doomed fate. Anyway, it was hugely refreshing, as you can imagine, to see a totally different type of woman. Her tennis dresses were a bit 'fluffy', but her butchness shone through. I wanted to be like her, or even to become her, but it seemed impossible for me to 'unprettify' myself, so I admired her instead. I badly wanted muscles and strength, but didn't think I could ever change my physique. (Plump, huge tits, huge hips.) Hers was a body I desperately wanted for myself. I thought my life would be so much better if I had her body instead of mine.

Miranda describes how Martina's masculinity provided a role model for her own developing teenage lesbian identity, and how she admired the subversion of the signs of conventional femininity that Martina achieved through this masculine image. That fans identified with this quality in Martina shows how masculinity is a clear indication of lesbianism for young women who want to come out as lesbians.

Zwerman suggests, as the above extract also implies, that the idea of difference, and otherness, clearly structured the media representation of Martina:

As it became increasingly clear that Navratilova was going to be Evert's top on-court challenger and that the two would be likely to contend against each other for the top singles titles for years to come, the tennis establishment had to figure out a way to market the show. They promoted the rivalry between Navratilova and Evert as a battle of opposites. Evert was cast as the favourite, the home-grown, all-American princess. Navratilova was the underdog, the intriguing but strange rough-around-the-edges alien, who had escaped from behind the Iron Curtain with only her tennis racket.[19]

In the mainstream media, then, Martina's 'masculinity' was continually viewed in opposition to Chris's 'femininity', even after Martina gained US citizenship. In order for Martina to become palatable to dominant culture, her Eastern European origins came to stand in for her lesbianism. However, as her career continued to prosper, dominant modes of representation became increasingly unsuccessful in attempts to secure normative messages about gender and sexuality in photographs of her.

As Martina's success on the international tennis circuit increased and she became somehow 'less foreign' (after gaining US citizenship in 1981, she became increasingly Americanized – bleaching her hair, patenting her rackets and other tennis accessories, and dating American girls), the strict gender order, perpetuated through the othering of Martina in relation to Chris, became less easy to maintain through her media representation. Representations of Martina began to circulate more widely, depicting her not only as a tennis player but also a tennis *star*. As I suggested above, lesbian stardom is structured by the contrasting discourses of idealization and ordinariness. I want to suggest, further, that the importance of masculinity in the consumption of pictures of Martina by her lesbian fans challenges the heterosexist connection of *femininity* to woman, and instead, proposes an alternative connection of *masculinity* to woman as both ideal and ordinary.

Serenading Stardom

It is important to examine how contemporary images of media personalities such as kd lang conform to, but also resist, codes of representation developed in relation to Hollywood stars of the 1940s and 1950s. In order to understand the gender contradictions at play in the representations of kd it is helpful to compare a photograph of her that appeared in Victoria Starr's biography with one of Rita Hayworth that was used by Jackie Stacey in her book *Star Gazing*, where she examines the female audiences of female film stars of the 1940s and 1950s.[20] (It may seem incongruous to incorporate an analysis of a photograph of Rita Hayworth in a study of lesbian stardom, however, it is useful to show how kd's image compares with that of a conventionally feminine Hollywood star.) Both images employ the conventional Hollywood code of the facial close-up: in film, television and, increasingly, music the face has a central function in the construction of a star's visual gendered desirability, and is seen as a way to represent the 'inner soul' or personality. In particular, the facial close-up is often used in order to generate meanings about masculinity or femininity in a star image, and, subsequently, a particular audience identification with that image. Stuart Ewen references Hortense Powdermaker on the close-up: 'Hortense Powdermaker, writing on the star system of Hollywood, spoke of the "close-up" shot as a monument to intimacy; each pore, each line on the face, each expression becomes memorized as the possession of the spectator.'[21]

Specific lighting techniques and the developing and printing processes can be utilized in the construction of femininity and masculinity as natural attributes of women and men. Traditionally, soft lighting and a coquettish or shy pose are frequently used to imply femininity, whereas sharp light and dark shadows, often accompanied by the highlighting of stubble, signifies masculinity. For a feminine image low-contrast photographic paper might be used, whereas a more masculine image maybe printed on a high-contrast paper. In order to establish suitably different meanings of gender, low-contrast paper hides any facial blemishes, reinforcing normative messages about a smooth feminine face; whereas high-contrast paper highlights imperfections and blemishes and creates a more rugged, scarred and stubbled masculine appearance.[22]

In the two facial close-up photographs I wish to discuss here kd lang and Rita Hayworth are both leaning energetically across the frame of the picture. kd is pictured wearing a masculine suit, has short spiky hair and is clutching an award. She also sports a wide smile, showing her teeth. The picture of Rita Hayworth is a publicity photo, so she is perfectly made up, and is also smiling confidently to reveal her sparkling white teeth. Often in facial close-ups of filmstars, and more recently pop stars, the hair is swept back and up from the head to reveal a happy and smiling face. The swept-back hair is particularly suggestive of an 'honest' and innocent character, as the image of hair across the face may suggest concealment.

There are also significant differences between the ways in which these two photographs may be read. Rita Hayworth has long, flowing hair and her low-cut dress reveals her cleavage; she is also clearly wearing make-up and has plucked eyebrows, creating a smoothness that is further enhanced by soft lighting. In contrast, kd's shirt is buttoned up to the neck, and neither her haircut nor any of her clothes suggest femininity. It is thus possible to read differences between these two photographs in terms of gender: kd's gender becomes unassimilable into the conventional framework of photographic display that characterizes representations of femininity in the mainstream media. With her very short hair, apparent lack of make-up and clothes that cover her body up to the neck, she could easily be mistaken for a man. Further, light and dark tones contrast to reveal shadows under her eyes and over the rest of her face, making her appear somewhat rugged.

This next quote illustrates the importance of kd's face to her lesbian fans:

I fantasize about having sex with her, but I think mostly about her face. I saw her body in *Salmonberries*, but it didn't really make any impression on me – even though I am very into a woman's body when I am having a relationship with her, I would still fancy her and find her attractive no matter what shape her body was. I concentrate more on how lovely her face is – so boyish and androgynous. She looks like a boy but is a girl, that ambiguity is very appealing, like the 'naughty' feeling of holding hands in public with someone everyone assumes is your boyfriend, but is your girlfriend.

(Sal)

Here, we can see how the appeal of kd's face lies in its challenge to femininity. The 'naughtiness' of this gender ambiguity is tied to the disruption of gender norms in representations of kd. In a recent issue of *Rolling Stone*, kd is pictured on her motorbike.[23] Significantly, and paradoxically, this picture affirms the connection of 'masculinity' to 'woman'. Straddling her powerful bike, kd smiles, and rests her arms leisurely on the handlebars. A straggling lock of hair strategically hangs down over her face, signalling a very low-key, relaxed atmosphere, which contrasts sharply with her more strictly 'posed' photographs. Her 'chunky' necklaces, bracelets and rings sparkle against the polished metal of the motorbike, symbolizing a hard, machine-like masculinity that contrasts with more conventional 'feminine' styles of jewellery.

This kind of photograph is reminiscent of earlier representations of male idols such as Marlon Brando. Brando became an iconic figure representing rugged, yet subversive, masculinity in the 1950s and 1960s; the textual similarities between the photograph of kd lang in *Rolling Stone* and the popular iconographic image of Marlon Brando leaning across his motorbike wearing a leather cap and a leather jacket are staggering. This image of kd illustrates how the mainstream media cannot constrain her identity within conventional codes of representation which rest on the connection of 'femininity' to 'woman'.

There is an ease of identity which shines forth through the realist conventions used in the documentary style photograph of kd lang in *Rolling Stone*. In *The Burden of Representation*, John Tagg discusses the documentary photographic style and its operation through the discourse of 'truth':

documentary came to denote a discursive formation which was wider by far than photography alone, but which appropriated photographic technology to a central and privileged place within its rhetoric of immediacy and truth. Claiming only to 'put the facts' directly or vicariously, through the report of 'first hand experience', the discourse of documentary constituted a complex strategic response to a particular moment of crisis in Western Europe and the USA – a moment of crisis not only of social and economic relations and social identities but, crucially, of representation itself: of the means of making the sense we call social experience.[24]

In documentary style, then, the photograph of kd on her bike plays upon the incongruity of the relationship of 'masculine' to 'woman', and lesbian identity is made to seem natural. This is at odds with the social unacceptability of lesbianism, and the way in which lesbianism is seen as an unnatural sexual deviance in western society. This paradox between natural and unnatural produces a tension of meanings about lesbianism, highlighting the social processes through which it has become demonized as a perversion in popular folklore. In the easy, natural picture of kd hanging over her motorbike handles, lesbianism may be read as equally ordinary and natural, perhaps leading the viewer to think all the more about the way that lesbians are oppressed via uneasiness, unnaturalness and non-ordinariness.

It is important to point out here that the cultural production of identity rests to a significant degree on *how* images are read. In an article on the 1960s Pop artist Andy Warhol, Robin Marriner references the work of Ludwig Wittgenstein, suggesting that the way Warhol appropriates popular imagery in his work (the face of Marilyn, for example, in Warhol's 1962 *Marilyn Monroe Diptych*) is radical because he illustrates Wittgenstein's theory about two ways of seeing an image:

What is being suggested ... (in opposition to the frequent claim that we, or at least they i.e. the masses see images as 'unmediated', 'transparent' representations of reality) is that all images are marks deployed on a surface, and that we know that. In looking at an image, in one sense of see (Wittgenstein's first sense) what we see are marks on a surface, but we also see (in Wittgenstein's second sense) (provided we have the requisite skills/knowledges) those marks as Marilyn Monroe, or a Car Crash or whatever. In our normal engagement with these images in the contexts from which they have been drawn our interest is in what we see in the second sense of see, that is, with what we see these marks as, with what these images are 'of', not with the marks themselves. Warhol uses sufficient of the conventions of representational mark making that the images can be seen as Marilyn etc. but in using marks that go against those conventions our attention is drawn to the marks themselves. That is, the works effect what is always potentially possible in relation to our looking at an image – that both 'objects of sight' are brought to our attention.[25]

In the case of photographic representations of kd and Martina, it is not the 'marks' that forestall a 'spontaneous' seeing of 'Martina' or 'kd', but rather the *knowledge* that they are *lesbian stars*. In other words the lesbian consumer is somewhat 'stunned' to see representations which portray *lesbians* as talented stars and successful media personalities, as we are more accustomed to lesbian invisibility and negative representation. This paradox forces the reader first to notice the images as *images-of-lesbians*, and secondly, read them *as* 'kd' or 'Martina'. This quote from a lesbian fan of both Martina and kd highlights how these lesbian idols are consumed with the knowledge of how unusual it is for lesbians to reach such heights of stardom:

> I guess deep down if these women weren't lesbians I wouldn't hold them in such high regard, but I think it's good they have the limelight that they deserve, I'm sure they have opened the way to many more great lesbian stars, in whatever career they choose.
>
> *(Kim)*

Thus, the more 'spontaneous' response Marriner describes as Wittgenstein's 'second sense of see' is forestalled when fans see lesbian stars as 'famous lesbians', and, through this radical separation of image and referent, attention is drawn to the processes of cultural representation which usually mark lesbianism as a deviance.

The naturalization of identity in images of kd and Martina that I have discussed in this section occurs through the gender contradictions in the idealization of the lesbian, specifically through the interconnection of 'masculine' and 'woman'. Therefore, in my view, this re-naturalization is deconstructive insofar as the idealization of gendered and sexed identities in these images in no way confirms a heterosexual matrix, but rather produces lesbian identity as ideal – an identity entirely at odds with heterosexuality.

In the Picture: Inhabiting Stardom

In any analysis of gender it is crucial to acknowledge that the processes in western culture by which masculinity and femininity are reproduced through representations of the categories of 'man' and 'woman' draw on particular discourses. In recent theory biological discourse has been a focal point for the deconstruction of binary models of sex, gender, race and ethnicity. Knowledges about biology in contemporary western society reinforce heterosexual genders of 'masculine' and 'feminine' in relation to the categories of 'male' and 'female' through the notion of 'sex': 'something' happening *inside* the bodies of individuals is said to determine the basis on which social meanings are built.

This 'something' has taken on different meanings over time, but more recently has been linked to some kind of 'scientifically traceable' criteria, such as genetic coding. This idea of 'something being inside' which determines the social meanings and functions of the body of an individual lies at the crux of biological determinism, which holds the body, marked as 'male' or 'female', to be the determinant of gender characteristics. Biological determinism is a form of essentialism which assumes that the body is the pre-existent referent for the cultural inscription of meanings about identity, such as gender (but also race and ethnicity[26]).

Examining the representation of Martina and kd as lesbian stars must involve understanding the significance of 'the body' as a topic of investigation in recent feminist theory. Judith Butler, in *Bodies that Matter*, has raised important questions concerning the construction of gender through a body that is marked by 'sex'. Butler suggests that theoretical work needs to be carried out on the status of the body in contemporary western belief systems in order to clarify the relationship of sex to gender:

> The discourse of 'construction' that has for the most part circulated in feminist theory is perhaps not quite adequate to the task at hand. It is not enough to argue that there is no prediscursive 'sex' that acts as the stable point of reference on which, or in relation to which, the cultural construction of gender proceeds. To claim that sex is already gendered, already constructed, is not yet to explain in which way the

69

'materiality' of sex is forcibly produced. What are the constraints by which bodies are materialized as 'sexed', and how are we to understand the 'matter' of sex, and of bodies more generally, as the repeated and violent circumscription of cultural intelligibility?[27]

In this section I will illustrate how bodies signify in particular ways, with reference to both gender and sex, in specific photographic representations of kd and Martina. I hope it will become clear how the 'materiality' of sex, posited by Butler, is forcibly produced to serve dominant interests and knowledges through particular modes and processes of cultural representation, and how readings of specific images of kd and Martina, as lesbian idols, produce meanings that are paradoxical to the traditional heterosexual logic of gender and its relationship to a determining sexed body.

From Forehand to Forearm: Martina's 'Perfect Lesbian Body'

Martina's body is significant in relation to the questions Butler asks, as representations of Martina may destabilize the heterosexual relationship between gender and sex which she examines. In the following section, then, I will look at the ways in which Martina is represented through codes of bodily masculinity.

Much significance is placed on Martina's body, or rather the 'spectaclization' of certain *parts* of her body, in both mainstream and, increasingly, lesbian-produced media. Martina's arm is the central feature of the photograph on the cover of this book. Published in the sports section of *The Times* in 1994, the shot of her arm reaching upwards in a victory gesture is reminiscent of the Statue of Liberty and, hence references her status as a fully fledged American tennis star. The photograph is also shot in a way which sheds light upon a reading of Martina as an object of desire. The representations of Martina's muscular arms reference a form of masculinity privileged in sporting images of men. The heavy jewellery on her fingers and wrist reinforces this reading of masculinity, as was the case in the image of kd lang I discussed earlier.

A similar emphasis on Martina's hands and arms occurs in a photograph on the cover of the February 1996 issue of the US lesbian magazine *Curve*. In this image Martina thrusts her left forearm towards the camera and clenches her fist in victory. Her mouth is open as she shouts out her pleasure at winning. The veins on her arms are clearly visible, and the muscles in her arm are firm. The fact that this photograph has been used for the front cover of a specifically lesbian glossy magazine highlights the way in which Martina is idolized in lesbian culture; indeed, the caption at the foot of the picture, 'Martina moves ahead and takes control', signifies that she is adored for her lesbian identity and strength of character, as much as for her muscular body.

These images illustrate how recent representations of Martina have placed an increased emphasis on her physicality, but also on the fragmentation of her body. (In the next chapter I will discuss these particular photographs in terms of the discourse of fetishism.)

In responding to these images which emphasize Martina's strength, an audience is required to draw both on knowledges about traditional representations of masculinity and knowledges about Martina's lesbian identity. The implementation of these knowledges, then, may indeed construct Martina's identity as a 'masculine lesbian'. Sarah Schulman has argued that photographic images of lesbians and gays in the straight and lesbian and gay media are becoming increasingly indistinguishable in the 1990s:

> it is hard to ignore the increasing similarity between the mainstream media and the gay press' versions of gay life. To some extent this dissolution of oppositionality does seem rooted in the increased commodification of homosexual life and the corporate identification of an openly gay consumer.[28]

The following quotes from two of Martina's lesbian fans illustrate the importance of Martina's body in her construction as a lesbian idol:

> I liked all of her body, but especially her hands. As a piano player I always notice people's hands, and can fall in love with someone for their hands even if it's the only part of their body I find attractive. Her hands are muscular and veined – my favourite type of hands. They look so strong and capable, she seems someone I could depend on because of her hands, if we were lovers. ... If I meet a woman with strong hands I think she must be a good lover. I'm sure Martina is very good in bed – I imagine her to be very butch, in command, but also gentle. I don't think she would be a 'do-me queen' who would just lie back and wait!
>
> (Miranda)

Her muscles are outrageously gorgeous, her physique is so beautiful, her legs are so sexy and strong and her arms and hands are just so muscular and gorgeous. Every inch of her body is wonderful and sexy – I suppose she has, for me, the perfect lesbian body ...

(Sadie)

It is particularly significant that this form of representation of Martina *fragments* her body by placing an emphasis on her arms and hands. The fragmentation of the female body, in advertising images for example, has been the subject of much feminist debate over the past two decades. The partializing of the female form to sell products has been criticized by feminists for reducing 'woman' to a body part. In *Star Gazing* Jackie Stacey discusses how the star's fragmented and commodified body has been a highly charged area of analysis in feminist theory: 'the fragmentation and commodification of the female body has been a source of much feminist debate about the specificity of women's alienation and oppression'.[29] However, the valid criticism of much sexist-motivated representation presumes a male consumer for such images. Stacey herself goes on to suggest, however, that this fragmentation provides pleasure for female spectators. It is therefore important to examine how the partializing of Martina's body may be understood in terms of lesbian consumers.

It is important to situate such a discussion within an understanding of the importance of the difference between the 'fragment' and the 'whole'. Stuart Ewen argues how the representation of fragmented bodies reinscribes the identity of photographic models as 'whole' for the reader of the photograph:

In order to depict the 'dream of wholeness', fragmentation is often necessary. In the profession of photographic modelling, a model is often selected for the *perfection* of a particular part of the body. Danielle Korwin, the founder and owner of Parts Models, Inc., proudly proclaims, 'Yes, we do handle all body parts. Everything from finely manicured hands and feet to pouting lips, weathered hands, even models with two differently colored eyes.' In the photographic presentation of style and beauty, these parts become the building blocks of a complete image.

In the pursuit of this ideal, photographers regularly draw upon an inventory of disembodied parts, in order to construct the semblance of wholeness.[30]

Thus, it is possible to see how the photographic practices of stardom have recently made intertextual use of the conventions of advertising photography. However, in relation to Ewen's point about the construction of wholeness, I would like to suggest that viewing lesbian identity as 'whole' is problematic because of the way that lesbian identity is unsanctioned by heterosexually privileged culture and its codes of representation. Mainstream codes of representation which construct the dream of wholeness that Ewen describes have never inscribed a lesbian identity as 'whole' in the way they have inscribed a heterosexual identity as 'whole'. It is therefore helpful to return to Stacey's arguments about the way the fragmentation of female stars is consumed by female spectators. Indeed, Stacey highlights the possibility of identification precisely on the grounds of a fragmentation of the body, an argument which supersedes the idea that the body is fragmented in order to see it as whole:

> The whole body of the female star is a commodity, but the parts of her body (hair, legs, face) and the parts of her face (eyes, nose, mouth) and the parts of her eyes (colour, lashes, eyebrows) are also commodified. The female star's body is thus infinitely commodifiable and ... spectators attached immense significance to particular body parts.[31]

It seems, then, that although wholeness of identity or subjectivity is often socially and culturally denied women, the consumption of feminine and lesbian identities is nevertheless accomplished in this particularly pleasurable consumption of fragmentation in the star context.

In the cover image for this book, Martina has just thrown a ball and is about to serve, her open mouth revealing teeth which glint white in the shadows of the image, representative perhaps of her animalistic hunger for success. This animalism, as I described earlier, emphasizes the physical functions of her body drawing her image even further away from traditional notions of femininity. In written representations of Martina, animalism, monstrousness and the hunger for success are also linked to ideas of sporting perfection gained through a 'masculine' body. The

73

following two extracts illustrate how Martina is idolized by her lesbian fans for these qualities:

> I think Martina has done a lot for gay and lesbian relations throughout the world. I think society is beginning to accept us, slowly but surely and I think some of this is down to Martina. Not only has she done wonders for the game of tennis, but wonders for me, especially this year (1994). I learned a great lesson from her during this year's Wimbledon – if you want something bad enough you'll fight for it. Martina's aim was to reach the final in her retirement year and she did it ...
>
> *(Kim)*

> Every time I saw her on court I admired her more and more – her grace, speed, athleticism, talent – she played awesome tennis – and I considered her more attractive each time.
>
> *(Lisa)*

Adrienne Blue has written about Martina's sporting prowess: 'On court, Martina let the well-tuned machine that was her body do its precision work',[32] and later notices that when she won a particular match at Wimbledon, she had 'finally shown the killer instinct'.[33] Blue also states that, in a subsequent Wimbledon final when Martina had been beaten by Steffi Graf, that Graf, 'whom Martina regards as her great rival ... had been a giant killer'.[34] In this use of the language of machinery and monstrousness we are given a picture of Martina as a machine-like powerful force reminiscent of the androids or cyborgs that inhabit science-fiction films such as *The Terminator*[35] or *Robocop*.[36]

This idea of Martina as a machine interconnects with the idea of lesbianism as a threat to the heterosexual gender order through the redeployment of masculinity in a lesbian context. In the films cited above, creations such as the Terminator or the malfunctional Robocops spread destruction and danger throughout the hyper-technological society that created them. The threat of lesbianism to the heterosexual gender order is perhaps similar. In the production and subsequent oppression of certain social groups, heterosexist discourses create potentially dangerous identities.[37]

An image which forms part of an advert for the Rainbow Card (the lesbian and gay credit card), published on the inside cover of the February

1996 issue of *Curve*, exemplifies this idea of Martina as a machine. Schulman[38] argues that the mainstream media, by marketing to lesbians and gays, are constructing the lesbian and gay identity as a new upper-class and privileged consumer group, so distracting attention from lesbian and gay oppression. The use of Martina's image in this advertisement is significant, as she certainly represents one of the more economically privileged lesbians.

In the Rainbow Card advert Martina is represented pulling an enormous cog on a large industrial machine. Bending and straining, she is clearly the motivating force which makes the central cog in this machine turn. She is wearing a black swimming costume, or leotard, and the muscles on her arms and hands are highlighted, as are those on her well-tuned muscular thighs. Her head is bowed as she directs her attention to the task in hand in a display of strength and concentration that is characteristic of her sporting career.

This image references knowledges about Martina as a fighting machine on the tennis court, but the slogan's imperative to 'Get it. Use it', which primarily is asking the reader to get a Rainbow Card, also refers to the way Martina has used her fame to benefit the lesbian and gay community.

The various representations of Martina's body as incredibly strong, but also monstrous and machine-like, enable the production of meanings about a particularly *embodied* masculinity in relation to pictures of her. This relates to Ewen's theory about how the construction of masculinity in late capitalist society is achieved via a notion of the 'hard body':

> The machine, with its indefatigable 'arms of steel', emerges as the prototype for virility, the mould from which the *new man* will be cast. If the idealized conception of the female body has provided a locus for the articulation of modern structures of value, the 'masculine physique' has been the tablet on which modern conditions of work, and of discipline, have been inscribed.[39]

Ewen goes on to describe the daily routine of 'Raymond H', a 34-year-old middle manager in a large New York City investment firm. Ewen provides this example to illustrate the correlation of 'masculinity' to 'machine':

> If the body ideal he seeks is *lean*, devoid of fatty tissue, it is also *hard*. 'Soft flesh', once a standard phrase in the American erotic lexicon, is

now – within the competitive, upscale world he inhabits – a sign of failure and sloth. The hard shell is now a sign of achievement, visible proof of success in the 'rat race'. The goal he seeks is more about *looking* than *touching*.[40]

Certain representations of Martina may be read in terms of this idea of the 'hard body': the 'precision work' of tennis that Zwerman describes Martina's body *doing* places an emphasis on work and profit, instilled in a late capitalist perspective on machinery and technology.

Lesbian stardom, then, may seem to make lesbianism normal and natural (as in the *Rolling Stone* photograph of kd), but equally, in this representation of Martina as machine-like and monstrous, it must change the ways that we think about the dominant discourses of the natural and how they work to subordinate lesbians. For example, are we witnessing the naturalization of lesbian identity in this star process via the very ideas of monstrosity, perversion and unnaturalness which for so long have been used to portray lesbianism as deviant in western culture?

Resurfacing the Body

I have suggested that representations of Martina may be read in terms of 'masculinity' and the language of animalism, drive, hardness and machinery. By contrast, representations of kd lang may be read in terms of a *deferral* of the body through a notion of *style*. The social arena of sport places a great deal of emphasis on the physicality in the representations of its sporting stars. However, kd is much more a media personality than Martina, and, as such, is represented more often through codes and conventions associated with the general representation of media and popular singing stars.

In contemporary western society these codes and conventions rely on understandings of depthlessness or superficiality which recall theories about postmodernist culture (I argued this point earlier in relation to the sporting stardom of André Agassi). In this section I examine how 'the body' is controversially gendered in representations of kd in relation to this idea of superficiality. To this end I will also look at notions of postmodernist culture.

Late twentieth-century society has witnessed rapid advancements in the areas of telecommunications and the manufacture of goods. These technological advancements have, in turn, created a rapid worldwide turnover in the production and consumption of saleable items used for day-to-day living – clothes, fashion accessories, shoes, cars, household products, magazines, technical objects such as computer software and hardware, music systems, televisions as small as wristwatches, wristwatches as complex as computers, VCRs, 'Sky' and satellite television, and more recently, the computer-based Internet. The Internet provides numerous opportunities for computer literates to take part in interactive practices such as global communication, games, debates and also, of course, virtual sex (including gay, lesbian and 'queer' discussion space and sex). The mass commodification of culture in late twentieth-century society is geared to rapidly changing styles – lifestyles, fashion styles and product design. It has been argued that this phenomenon of rapid change has had the effect of 'flattening out' cultural life and making superficiality a definitive aspect of social experience.[41]

Mike Featherstone examines the importance of surface in our lives in his analysis of what he terms 'postmodernity'. He briefly describes the theoretical writings of Jean Baudrillard and Frederic Jameson and their definitions of postmodernity. Both of these theorists, he argues, stress the significance of forms of media representation:

> Baudrillard ... stresses that new forms of technology and information become central to the shift from a productive to a reproductive social order in which simulations and models increasingly constitute the world so that the distinction between the real and appearance becomes erased.[42]

Featherstone goes on to suggest that Jameson's position stresses the 'transformation of reality into images and the fragmentation of time into a series of perpetual presents'.[43]

Baudrillard's perspective seems to encompass the notion that meanings are forever shifting and therefore become increasingly divested of importance by social groups. Notably, Featherstone claims that Baudrillard theorizes away 'the social' as a field of struggle for groups of individuals:

> Baudrillard's ... depiction of a postmodern simulational world is based upon the assumption that the development of commodity production coupled with information technology have led to the 'triumph of signifying culture' which then reverses the direction of determinism, so that social relations become saturated with shifting cultural signs

to the extent that we can no longer speak of class or normativity and are faced by 'the end of the social'.[44]

Featherstone rejects Baudrillard's 'end of the social' theory because it focuses only on the intellectual descriptions of late twentieth-century society and does not take into account what is happening between people in everyday life. Instead, he insists: 'we should focus upon the actual cultural practices and changing power balances of those groups engaged in the production, classification, circulation and consumption of postmodern cultural goods'.[45] Postmodernist culture is often viewed in contrast to 'actual cultural practices'. I wish to examine meanings of gender in relation to this tension between postmodernist superficiality and the cultural practices involved in reading images of kd. In other words, how does this postmodernist idea of changing surface styles bear on meanings made via the consumption of lesbian stars?

kd lang is often depicted in highly stylistic poses typical of any fashion magazine. Relying on contemporary visual codes which represent women as androgynous, but also 'boyish', her appearance is often ambiguous in terms of gender. Therefore, the construction of her image relies on two different notions of masculinity – that which represents men as 'masculine', and that which represents women as 'boyish'. An image which encapsulates this boyish, androgynous look, popular in the mainstream media, was published in Victoria Starr's biography of kd, and shows kd with slicked back hair and casual yet stylish clothes cuddling a little dog.

These ideas of masculinity, however, depend on particular ways of covering the body and lighting the face. The photographic codes used in slick, glossy advertising images, which represent men as masculine and women as boyish, highlight a deferral of the body in contemporary culture which has pushed the importance of style *per se* to the forefront of the consideration of *image*. However, paradoxically, due to knowledges about lesbian identity and kd that an audience brings to representations of her, the meanings made here involve the contradictory idea that a superficial image refers to an identity of 'lesbian' which is in fact deeply embodied and 'lived out' in the social field.

The 'boyish woman' image is rendered innocuous (that is, not signifying lesbianism) when used in representations of heterosexual female stars or models, and thus poses no real threat to the heterosexual matrix of gender and sex. Images of kd which are constructed in this way make clear the processes through which heterosexual identities are re-secured and re-naturalized through a 'play' with opposing, or 'other', identities. Such play highlights the impermanence of this opposing identity, but also reconstitutes the sense of a grounding heterosexual identity behind the play: a place to play *from*.

However, having said this, the construction of kd lang as 'boyish' in one sense also satirizes these representational codes and the reproduction of an ideal heterosexual identity. Dominant representations of hetero-sexuality in postmodernist terms often operate through *playing* or *flirting* with controversial, and subordinate, identities, such as that of 'the lesbian'. However, when a famous and real lesbian, such as kd, is represented along the same lines, the 'boyish woman' image suddenly becomes deeply problematic – as an image of a boyish kd lang most definitely signifies lesbianism.

'Identity play' is also utilized in these boyish images of kd lang, but at one level this results in an ironic meaning, because a knowledge of kd's lesbian identity is brought to the image by a lesbian, or, indeed, a straight audience. The lesbian *body* of kd lang, then, rather than being rendered meaningless, is resurfaced with knowledges about her lesbian identity which reveal the regulatory ground of heterosexual identity surrounding the idea of the boyish woman. kd's stylish hair and clothes, for example, reflect the construction of lesbian identities through a particular use of 'masculine' dress codes, and the way she cuddles the dog reflects a trend in mainstream advertising imagery to photograph models with cats, dogs and even leopard and lion cubs; however in this picture the use of the dog also reminds lesbian readers of kd's love for animals and her anti-vivisectionist politics. Thus my interpretation of this image of kd illustrates how popular advertising imagery and lesbian-specific knowledges combine to produce a challenge to a dominant heterosexual deployment of the notion of the boyish woman.

A photograph of kd published in *Mojo* in December 1993[46] is particularly representative of the renewed focus on the body in the fashion world, and in contrast to the image discussed above attempts to represent kd as decidedly feminine. In this picture kd's shirt is unbuttoned down to her waist revealing her black lacy underwear and the upper contours of her breasts. This atmospheric black and white image references many iconic visual experiences, from deserted outdoor shots in small Mexican towns in spaghetti westerns, to black and white Calvin Klein cologne advertisements. kd leans back against a rundown whitewashed building, half closing her eyes against the bright sunlight that beats down on her bare face and cleavage, her hair is slicked back, and slightly longer than in those early cowboy days. However, kd's prominent jaw line and large facial features, far from representing conventional codes of feminine beauty, are, by contrast, complicit with mainstream understandings of masculinity. Yet again, such a representation highlights a particularly embodied image that challenges heterosexual definitions of gender difference that are determined by a body marked by sex.

Rather than reinforcing meanings of gender and sex within a heterosexual matrix, such images of kd lang's female body have produced even more contradictory messages about gender and sex. Far from securing kd within a 'woman's' body, they have only highlighted the instability of the category of 'woman'. Clearly this picture cannot stand alone; in fact, meanings can only be produced in relation to an image via intertextual relationships between the image, further representations and audience knowledges. Gender contradictions in other photographs of kd lang (and in images of Martina) resurface in meanings produced in relation to the textual organization of this photograph of kd. Hence, the representation of 'woman', and the overall connection of 'woman' to 'femininity', comes under a kind of scrutiny unprecedented within mainstream visual cultural production. In this context, it is useful to examine the ways in which journalists interpret such representations. This extract from Leslie Bennets's interview with kd in *Vanity Fair* illustrates the contradictory meanings of gender and sex categories that persist in readings of photographs of her:

> Looking at her right now one could easily mistake her for a very cute, smooth-faced boy, despite the assortment of silver bracelets on her wrist. She is wearing ripped jeans, a white T-shirt with a denim shirt over it, and those rubber boots. It takes a while to realize that there is a quintessentially womanly body inside those clothes. 'Her figure is a revelation!' exclaimed one critic after seeing lang's nude scene in *Salmonberries*.[47]

This quote also illustrates how the speculation around kd's gender ambiguity, which lies at the root of her appeal, extends to a wider audience than just lesbians. Thus, the paradoxical connection of woman to masculinity in relation to the image of kd has been noticed by the wider culture.

So far in this chapter I have argued that reading photographic images of Martina and kd in specific ways challenges heterosexual gender difference. I have suggested that the representation of lesbian identity through the discourse of stardom has produced paradoxical interrelations of sex and gender meanings which radically undermine the heterosexual correlation of masculine to man to male, and of feminine to woman to female. I have shown how reading pictures of kd and Martina in certain ways may bring into question the relationship of particular sexed bodies to particular genders with particular gender attributes, and, indeed, may also question just what it means to 'be' a 'woman' or a 'man'.

In the last part of this chapter I will examine further images of Martina and kd in order to examine how contradictory meanings about sex and gender may affect how we think about race and ethnic identity. I also wish to highlight the processes by which dominant and oppressive meanings about race and ethnicity are constructed through particular modes of representation which have an implicit, and causal, relationship to sex and gender.

'A Race Apart': Ethnicity and the Lesbian Idol

In this section I will attempt to demonstrate how diverse ethnic and racial identities are maintained through representation, examining also how meanings about ethnic and racial identities which may be produced in relation to representations of these lesbian idols may seem contradictory and unable to be constrained under the premise of binary difference.

In order to proceed, it is important to clarify meanings of 'race' and 'ethnicity'. In an edition of *Feminist Review* which contains a discussion of such definitions and meanings Avtar Brah and Kum-Kum Bhavnani both succinctly point out that the scientific category of race is inherently contradictory, with no logical biological validity. Bhavnani argues that 'Race is a concept which has no biological basis. ... All the criteria which apparently assert the reality of 'race', such as hair type, shape of face, blood group, are shown not to be discrete across human populations and genepools.'[48] Brah makes a similar point, maintaining that the concept of race references [a] historically variable nexus of social meanings. That is to say that it is a social construction. Any number of markers – colour, physiognomy, culture, gene pools – may be summoned as signifiers of 'race'. Certain forms of racism will highlight biological characteristics as indicators of supposed 'racial' difference.[49]

Race, then, is a concept which is based on fantasized criteria with no logical validity; therefore, it is critical to understand how ideas of nation and ethnicity often coincide to provide criteria for recognizing racial identity.

The concept of 'nation' interweaves with meanings of 'ethnicity' to establish ideas about race, racial difference and racism. Brah suggests that nationalisms, in practice, draw on the 'civic' and 'ethnic' elements in A. D. Smith's theory. She argues that Smith's 'civic' model should be viewed 'as the possession of a historic territory, a sense of a legal-political community that is subject to common laws and institutions, a presumption of legal and political equality among members of such a community, and identification with a common culture.'[50] She then claims that Smith's 'ethnic' concept of 'nation' 'emphasizes a common descent and ties based on kinship, vernacular languages, customs and traditions ...'.[51] Brah goes on to define 'ethnicity' via Frederik Barth's view that ethnic groups can be identified through the idea of *boundaries*,[52] arguing that his is a non-essentialist theory as it allows for shifts in meanings:

His definition has the merit of constructing ethnic groups in non-essentialist terms. For instance, processes of boundary construction, maintenance and dissolution vary over time. They are subject to the forces of socio-economic and political change. Since they are historical products bonds of ethnicity may shift in meaning, may be strengthened, weakened or dissolved, and they will have varied salience at different points in an individual's or group's biography.[53]

She asserts, further, that there are a range of specific criteria through which ethnic boundaries may be maintained:

These may include a belief in common ancestry, claims to a shared history that gives shape to feelings of shared struggles and shared destinies, attachment to a homeland which may or may not coincide with the place of residence, and a sense of belonging to a group with a shared language, religion, social customs and traditions.[54]

These analyses reveal how racisms feed on the interweaving meanings around national identity, boundaries of ethnicity and supposed biological signifiers of race. Brah's definitions are useful to me in my analysis of the representations of kd and Martina as they help to frame an understanding of how these representations may be consumed within the specific context of British lesbian culture.

In much contemporary theory it is widely held that notions of gender, class, sex, race, nation and ethnicity interconnect within and across diverse social contexts and political struggles. Bhavnani aptly clarifies this trend to look for historical and social specificity in order to understand cultures, and suggests that the use of the concept of *identity* may facilitate this kind of specificity:

> The problem with some approaches to multiculturalism ... is that they often work as if each 'group', whether defined according to religion, for example Muslims, or geographical origin, for example as coming from the continent of Africa, or linguistic heritage, for example as speaking 'Chinese', is homogenous in its composition. Such an approach not only by-passes the historical and political differences within such groups, but also side-steps the recognition that the groups contain class, gender and distinctions of sexuality within them. It is true, therefore, that culture is neither homogenous nor static, and that cultures are created through histories and politics. Therefore, identity may provide a boundary for definitions of culture which permits more fluidity and dynamism.[55]

However, even though Bhavnani stresses the importance of identity in clarifying cultural difference, in theorizing about lesbian identity it is easy to bypass questions of race and ethnicity and focus only on the potential radicality of the representations of kd and Martina's lesbian identity. However, the shifts in meanings around racial, national and ethnic identity which have occurred as a result of political, economic and cultural changes within Europe over the past few years have duly affected the ways in which people consume all kinds of cultural products and representations.

In this section I will suggest that the 'othering' of kd and Martina in terms of their 'masculine' gender and lesbian sexuality, foregrounds a lesbian identity, relegating ethnicity to a less important role in the construction of these stars, and in the consumption of identity that also takes place here. In other words, questions of race and ethnicity in readings of these lesbian idols are *concealed* by their identities as lesbians and the lesbian identity of a significant portion of their audience. My examination of how these idols are read in British lesbian culture is an attempt to contextualize consumption practices as much as possible in order to avoid universalist reasoning around the representation of lesbianism *per se*.

Judith Butler clarifies this issue of the concealment of other parts of identity in the constitution of a lesbian identity:

> There is no question that gays and lesbians are threatened by the violence of public erasure, but the decision to counter that violence must be careful not to reinstall another in its place. Which version of lesbian or gay ought to be rendered visible, and which internal exclusions will that rendering visible institute? ... If the rendering visible of lesbian/gay identity now presupposes a set of exclusions, then perhaps part of what is necessarily excluded is *the future uses of the sign.*[56]

Thus, visual representations of kd and Martina in the British mainstream media may be read in a way which re-idealizes whiteness through the *concealment* of ethnic specificity.

In order to analyse how the intersection of notions of gender, sex and ethnicity enable the production of Martina and kd as 'lesbian idols', it is important to ask two questions. First, in what ways may concealment or exclusion in representations of kd and Martina be read within a particularly British context? Second, how may this contextualized understanding of concealment radically problematize notions of gender, sexual, racial and ethnic identity which are premised on binary opposition at a wider level?

The Blonde Goddess
Martina defected from communist Czechoslovakia in 1975, and became a US citizen in 1981. The fact that Martina has had two nationalities (US and Czechoslovakian) but one 'homeland' and one 'ethnic heritage' (Czech) must play a central role not only in how she is represented in the mainstream media as a lesbian tennis star but also how these representations may be read in a specifically British context.

Significantly, Martina's lesbianism may be read in terms of both her nationalities, as lesbianism will signify differently in different national contexts. For example, as an Eastern European woman, as I have already argued, Martina may be read as a 'deviant masculinized Eastern European lesbian athlete'. However as a US citizen she may, alternatively, be consumed in an atmosphere of liberal democracy, where freedom of speech is valued, identity is fluid and lesbian and gay lifestyles are much more visible; in short, a society that reflects the contemporary western commodity culture of the 1990s, and one in which the notion of a particularly commodifiable lesbian culture is gaining increasing currency. A British lesbian audience will view Martina's two national identities, and her lesbianism, within a European context, but also within the context of a western commodity culture. These two contexts of the consumption of lesbian identity through representations of Martina will subsequently bear on knowledges about race, ethnicity and nation in relation to specific formations of lesbian identity in Britain.

An important focus for considering the ethnic identity of Martina, and how it is read in a British context, is an examination of representations of her in relation to ideas about 'whiteness'. The concept of 'whiteness' rather than 'racially other' identities has come under close scrutiny in contemporary cultural and feminist theory.[57] In fact many contemporary theorists have considered the examination of racial otherness to be a racist approach in itself, as it often leaves a notion of white identity unaddressed. All mainstream representations of women in western culture, in one way or another, draw on the idea that 'white' femininity is the ideal form of femininity. Bearing this in mind, how may exploring the consumption of Martina as a lesbian idol in Britain be helpful in understanding how whiteness is produced as ideal through gendered cultural representations?

Kum Kum Bhavnani suggests that the unification of Europe in 1993 underlined a hierarchical difference between European and non-European countries which further enhanced western superiority:

> under the guise of internationalism, there is a strengthening of nationalism, and it is this process which is presently occurring within EC countries. That is, that as the populations who live in these countries are being urged to be Europeans, and not lay claim to national identities such as being French, or Dutch, or German, so, this very 'European identity' strengthens the distinction between European and non-European. My argument is that in the process of removing borders among EEC countries, the border between EEC and non-EEC nations becomes symbolically and actually stronger.[58]

The division Bhavnani describes between European and non-European also relates to the concept of 'whiteness'. The dominance of European countries over non-European countries, in my view, involves the idea that Europeans are supposedly *racially* superior to non-Europeans – this 'superior race' being 'white'.

In this context, British consumers of representations of Martina may, in Butler's terms, *conceal* her national 'otherness' (as Czech) in an attempt to see her as generally 'white'. Importantly, the concealment, here, of national difference takes place through the assertion of *racial* difference: for most British consumers, Martina will always be more 'white' (that is, more 'like them') than she is American or Czech. Such is the position of racial politics in Britain at the moment. Thus, the political climate of a particular country at any given time is an essential factor in determining meanings of race, nation or ethnicity in relation to any given representation.

The following quote illustrates the part ethnicity plays in Martina's status as a lesbian idol:

> With her blonde hair she reminds me of sunshine, and it is good to think of such a fine human being in this world which seems to be going to the bad in so many ways.
>
> *(Margot)*

Here Margot explains that it is the qualities of 'blondeness' and 'goodness' that she admires about her idol. This is significant, because these two signifiers construct a white feminine ideal which is at odds with Martina's masculinity.

In his article 'White', Richard Dyer has examined 'whiteness' in relation to film representation, using the example of Marilyn Monroe to discuss how white femininity is represented through specific photographic techniques:

> I suspect that there is some very interesting work to be done on the invention of photography and the development of lighting codes in relation to the white face, which results in the technicist ideology that one sometimes hears of it being 'more difficult' to photograph black people. Be that as it may, it is the case that the codes of glamour lighting in Hollywood were developed in relation to white women, to endow them with a glow and radiance that has correspondences with the

transcendental rhetoric of popular Christianity. ... Of no woman star was this more true than Marilyn Monroe, known by the press at the time as 'The Body' ... her image is an inescapably and necessarily a white one.[59]

This construction of whiteness as *ideal* in western culture is important to my analysis of how Martina is consumed in terms of racial discourse. The construction of Martina as 'masculine', however, poses a problem when viewing Martina as a 'white woman', because, as I have argued throughout this chapter, representations of Martina may be read in a way which consistently undercuts and problematizes what it means to be a 'woman'.

Diane Hamer in an article entitled 'Netting the Press: Playing with Martina', discusses how Martina's coverage in the press contrasts with the portrayal of Judy Nelson. She illustrates how Judy's femininity is consolidated by repeated references to her *blondeness*, whereas Martina's equally blonde hair is never mentioned:

'Live-in companion, blonde mother-of-two, former beauty queen, divorced ... *Daily Star*, 16 June 1987'

'Live-in lover, blonde mother of two Judy Nelson, ex-beauty queen. *People*, 21 June 1987'

The use of 'blonde' here clearly signifies Nelson's heterosexual attractiveness. Note that Martina is never described as blonde. Clearly a quintessential femininity, signified by blondeness, does not fit the description of Martina the lesbian.[60]

Although Martina's blondeness is not specifically referenced by Hamer ('excluded' or 'concealed' in Butler's terms), it acts as an indicator of her whiteness according to the western Christian rhetoric of race that Dyer discusses in relation to Marilyn Monroe. As he argues, 'Blondeness, especially platinum (peroxide) blondeness is the ultimate sign of whiteness.'[61]

Hamer implies that the absence of references to Martina's blondeness indicates her masculinity, just as Judy's blondeness is connected to her femininity. Hamer is correct to point out how the idea of blonde femininity is used to construct Martina as a deviant woman in contrast to Judy. However, I would like to suggest that Martina's blondeness, far from being *cancelled out* by the fact that it is not commented on, creates an irresolvable contradiction for the mass media over the construction of meanings of race and ethnicity in relation to meanings of Martina's controversial 'lesbian masculinity'. Here, we can see how Butler's idea of concealment may highlight contradictions that are potentially unsettling for heterosexuality.

In newspaper articles Martina's blondeness may never be mentioned; however, in photographs of her it is strikingly apparent that she is blonde, and, moreover, that she *bleaches* her hair – something associated with typical feminine behaviour, similar to that of archetypal white actresses such as Marilyn Monroe, and more contemporary music idols such as Madonna. This contradiction between her actual appearance and what is written about her may suggest that her identity as masculine 'other' to both Judy Nelson and Chris Evert is far from an uncomplicated binary same/other difference. Once again, the representation of Martina's 'masculinity' radically interconnects with a definition of 'woman', and disrupts the hierarchical heterosexual sex/gender system.

At this point it is important to ask: when Martina is consumed as 'white', does the idea of western racial superiority undermine the challenge posed by her masculinity to the heterosexual gender/sex matrix? Again, Dyer's discussion of white femininity is relevant here, particularly his reference to the way in which white femininity is highlighted through 'the transcendental rhetoric of popular Christianity'.[62] Hence, we may read Martina as both masculine and as a 'white' blonde goddess figure. Thus her image draws on discourses used to reproduce stars as both masculine and feminine.

Further, in contrasts between Martina and Judy in the tabloid press, Martina's whiteness may be deferred in a divisive heterosexist attempt to dislodge her from the 'acceptability' she would gain through 'being white'. Indeed, it may follow that the category of 'whiteness' is not only premised on racial or ethnic signifiers, such as a common culture or language, a skin of a certain colour, specific DNA formation, and so on, but that 'being white' may have as much to do with being heterosexual, or being a feminine woman, or a masculine man, as anything else.

Returning to Bhavnani's suggestion that European identities have recently been strengthened in the context of the European unification of 1993, it seems plausible that bypassing Martina's whiteness in an attempt to conceal her membership of a dominant group and, hence, maintain

Martina lunges powerfully forward towards the ball
with her single-handed forehand.

Chris Evert gracefully stretches to play a shot
with her double-handed backhand.

kd lang

her social unacceptability, may, paradoxically, be accompanied by a move on behalf of white lesbians to *normalize* Martina's white identity *as* a dominant white identity. White lesbians may wish to secure Martina's white identity because of the division between white and non-white identities which has accompanied the increased domination of non-European countries by Europe. It is, at least, naive to believe that such racist motivation does not underlie specific forms of lesbian identification with white lesbian idols. The concealment of Martina's 'whiteness' by dominant forms of representation may be seen as significantly under-challenged within an predominantly 'white' Euro-American lesbian population.

The Evasion of Identity

The consumption of kd lang also produces contradictions which reveal the processes through which race and ethnicity are constructed in mainstream representations. The way that kd herself makes multiple claims on disparate racial, religious and ethnic identities makes it impossible for a consumer to 'fix' her identity within one particular race or ethnicity. Rather than *concealing* or *excluding* her race or ethnicity, as in the case of Martina, representations of kd *disperse* her ethnic identity, but in a way which locates her lesbianism as more central (as, indeed, was also the case with Martina). Therefore, lesbianism is made central to the identity of both of these idols: with regard to Martina, through a concealment of 'whiteness', and in relation to kd, through a dispersal of racial or ethnic identity.

In an interview with kd in *Rolling Stone* Mim Udovitch discusses kd's Jewish heritage:

> She's more than just a lesbian, feminist, vegetarian Canadian. She's also into Greenpeace. No, I'm just kidding. She's also Jewish. 'I'll tell you something,' she says, lying on the floor of her little house in the Hollywood hills, which contains a cluster of menorahs and dreidels. 'I was 24 before I even knew what a bagel was. But I loved Jewish culture, and my friends made me an honorary Jew.' lang recently found out her maternal great-grandmother was Jewish, and the laws of matrilineal descent being what they are, she says: 'Now I'm a real Jew. I was raised as a Christian for the first thirteen years. Who knew?'[63]

kd's claim to Jewishness represents a recent preoccupation with collecting ethnic identities. This idiosyncrasy reflects a wider romanticism with certain identities that have recently come to be seen as quaint or appealing. In particular, the way that kd proclaims 'Now I'm a real Jew' highlights how identities are temporally constructed. Rather than acknowledging that she was always Jewish (the biologically determinist view) she locates her acquisition of Jewishness at a particular point in time. Here, then, discourses of 'discovery' and romanticism combine to problematize understandings of what it means to 'be Jewish'.

A popular romance with Judaism seems particularly heightened in relation to this interview with kd because her identification as Jewish seems to rest on the acquisition of specific foods and cultural artefacts associated with the Jewish religion, such as bagels, dreidels and menorahs, rather than a belief in God, an emphasis which would be unacceptable from an orthodox Jewish position. This is significant in relation to Brah's discussion of ethnicity that I outlined earlier, and her contention that there are a range of criteria through which ethnic boundaries are forged and maintained. However, in my view, conflicts may arise over the authenticity of such criteria. For instance, seeing Judaism as an identity based on the eating of particular foods or the displaying of certain ornaments may produce antagonism amongst those who view Judaism as a belief in God and the upholding of a particular set of religious guidelines, or as a vital element of their historical and cultural identity.

In another article in the music and movie magazine, *Ikon*, kd's Jewishness is referenced by the interviewer, and kd herself, as an attractive identity, both for its rich musical heritage and as a sign of oppression, which is inferred to be 'trendy':

> lang has developed a crush on Judaism. 'My partner, Ben Mink, who is Hassidic, has always said, you know, you're an honorary Jew, cos I've had some sort of weird connection to the humour, and to the rhythm. Then, recently, I found out that I actually am Jewish, via my great-grandmother. There's a type of Jewish soul, in arts and in music, that I find common, like the way Benny Goodman played. ... But you know what it is, more than anything? Being from Canada, such a young culture, you grasp at any heritage you can.' And Judaism is quite symbolic and ritualistic, it has its own elaboration. 'And oppression.' She grins, stretches. 'Which is always nice for an artist.'[64]

Again kd's adoption of Jewish culture is tied to aspects she seems to see as dispensable, such as oppression. Her statement that to be oppressed is 'nice' for an artist relates, in this context to Jewish rather than lesbian oppression. Thus oppression becomes another way in which ethnicities may seem attractive or trendy; yet, ironically, it would be unthinkable for kd to assert that lesbian oppression is 'nice'.

Meanings of ethnicity in the consumption of representations of kd lang are further problematized when her identity is continually speculated upon in the media. In *Vanity Fair* Leslie Bennets lists kd's various ethnicities as 'part Sioux, part Dutch, with English and Irish thrown in, and a few months ago she found out she's even part German Jewish'.[65] However, in her biography, Starr notes that kd's father believes her Native American identity is not as fixed as she implies:

> Kathy has also said that she is part Sioux, an assertion that makes her father chuckle. 'Not Sioux – Cree,' he grins. 'An old uncle of mine once did our family tree and came to the conclusion that one of my grandmothers was part Cree. But I wouldn't put it down as a verified fact. It's true that I'm often mistaken for Cree, but we just kind of took his word for it and never really looked into it any further.'[66]

This inter-family disagreement about kd's Native American descent is significant because it highlights the importance of *authenticity* to definitions of race or ethnicity. If ethnic identities cannot be verified through biological signifiers of race such as skin colour, bone structure and particular facial and bodily characteristics, then different kinds of 'proof' are often sought, such as legal documents from which family trees may be established. Ironically, within dominant western cultures, where legal records of family history are commonplace, it has never really been popular to assert membership of a subordinated ethnicity, such as a Native American identity, through the use of legal documentation (although in the USA this is changing). Thus western notions of 'evidence' and 'proof', on which a western meaning of authenticity depends, are meaningless in relation to cultures in which different methods of establishing kinship, such as oral history, are employed.

For her lesbian fans, however, kd's ethnicities are accepted. To a certain extent this reflects how fans often assume that their idols can do no wrong, and believe everything they say; but it also relates to the wider attraction of being ethnically other within a lesbian community dominated by white lesbians and discourses of difference which privilege whiteness as the ideal. Tiffany writes:

> I have pictures of kd all over my bedroom wall. I especially collect pictures of her face. She has beautiful features: jet black hair, blue eyes fringed with dark eyelashes, straight nose, high cheekbones. She has incredibly noble features and wonderful bone structure. You can really see the Sioux in her. Her mouth is quite small but voluptuous nonetheless ...
>
> *(Tiffany)*

Butler's idea that the construction of identity is only possible through the concealment of other identities is evident in the film *Salmonberries*,[67] starring kd lang. In an article about this film[68] I have underscored this idea of concealment through arguing that the Native American identity of kd's character in the film is used as an 'ethnic backdrop' to her emerging lesbian identity, which then becomes more important to the narrative and, thus, successfully conceals a Native American ethnicity.

Both aspects of kd's character, Kotzebue, are kept radically separate by means of analogy: the discovery of Kotzebue's Native American identity progresses in a similar way to the discovery of her lesbian identity, and both employ several different narrative strategies, such as the use of symbolic jewellery, the confiding in a close female friend about her identity, and so on. Although the constructions of a Native American ethnicity and a lesbian sexuality interconnect at points in the narrative, they never lose their discreteness, so that, in the end, lesbianism is favoured at the film's highly romantic closure. Thus lesbian sexuality in this film is not represented as existing *alongside* a Native American identity, but, rather, 'white' lesbian identity is confirmed as the most important part of Kotzebue's identity. Further, this whiteness dominates through the process of naturalization – whiteness is seen as so natural that it appears not to be there at all.

The privileging of a white lesbian identity over a Native American lesbian identity in this film leaves us no clearer about *kd's* ethnicity. The urge to *know* someone's ethnicity certainly reflects a desire to categorize them as members of a specific social group for the purposes of identification, disidentification, and often in order to oppress them. This desire to establish kd's ethnicity is exemplified in the interviews she has given, where journalists and biographers have constructed her as a 'carrier' of many ethnicities. Such contradictory constructions of kd's identity highlight the concealment of one identity by another: she is *clearly* a lesbian, but not *clearly* anything else.

Sometimes, photographic images of kd utilize established representational codes of racial difference, for example those used in 1940s Hollywood photography. In such images, light and dark are deployed in a particular way, and suggest racial purity and impurity. In *Star Gazing* Jackie Stacey includes a quote from a fan which illustrates how Ava Gardner was constructed along the lines of racial difference: '"I adored Ava Gardner's dark magnetism, but knew I wasn't like that."'[69] In the accompanying photograph the background is dark, and a stark light is thrown on the face to highlight its whiteness in contrast to both the background and her dark eyes and eyebrows. The hair is also dark, at places blending in with the background. The way the hair encroaches onto the face of the star may also be read in terms of racial discourse: these stray locks of hair penetrating into the white face may symbolize the invasion of white territories by racial 'others'. Thus, even though we could argue that Ava Gardner is constructed as a 'white woman' through normative Hollywood codes of star representation, her stardom is produced through racial signifiers which construct her desirability as an exotic 'other'. This, to some extent, reveals how attempts to 'fix' classic female Hollywood stars as white icons in the 1940s and 1950s sometimes failed.

In an article in *Q* magazine kd lang is represented through a similar discourse of racial otherness.[70] In an accompanying photograph there is a dark background, against which kd stands, her hand resting on a table as she looks at the camera over rose-tinted spectacles. She is wearing a striped blazer, a maroon waistcoat and a neck-scarf. The caption accompanying the image reads: 'Ladies and gentlemen, welcome, if you will, that sartorially challenged repository of narrowly held views, the beloved and chameleonic queen of popular music, k.d. lang ...'.[71] Like her rose-tinted spectacles, kd is often represented in interviews as wearing ethnic identities like masks that she seems able to put on and off with ease. However, this image in *Q* constructs her as an exotic 'other', not in order to try and paradoxically re-establish her whiteness, as in the photograph of Ava Gardner, but in a way which references her own claims to multiple ethnicity. It is as if she is being *promoted* via racial otherness, a commodification which highlights how the notion of ethnicity is utilized in representational practices to produce 'kd lang' as a saleable item for consumption.

It is also important that kd lang has an ambiguous relationship to gender in contrast to Ava Gardner, but also in relation to Rita Hayworth, as both of these Hollywood stars are clearly represented as overtly feminine. As I argued in my analysis of images of Martina, 'whiteness' may indeed be about having a skin of a particular colour, or being of a particular ethnic group, but it is equally about following the heterosexual gender norms of that group. In other words, what prevents kd from being read as a 'white woman' may be her multiple claims on different ethnicities, and what excludes Martina from this definition may be a prioritization of lesbianism over whiteness; but it is also, crucially, their *masculinity*.

Conclusion

In this chapter I have suggested that the deployment of specific Hollywood-style representational codes in photographic images of kd and Martina has resulted in the idealism of lesbian identity. This idealization is particularly ironic, and, moreover, paradoxical, in light of the subordination and oppression lesbians experience in a hostile homophobic western culture. It is my argument that this idealization of lesbian identity deconstructs heterosexual domination by revealing the very processes through which heterosexual identities are made to seem ideal. I have argued this point in relation to Marriner's description of Warhol's artistic intervention into the process of consumption. In relation to photographic representations of kd and Martina, a lesbian or, indeed, a heterosexual, audience is so taken aback to see idealistic representations of famous lesbians in the mainstream media that they are unable to see the images 'spontaneously' as 'Martina' or 'kd'.

Readings of kd and Martina may problematize and challenge normative meanings of masculinity and femininity and the heterosexual connection of particular gender characteristics to a particularly sexed body. However, it is much more difficult to suggest that such readings may also challenge dominant meanings of race and ethnicity. What my analysis may do, however, is to illustrate how identity categories traditionally defined in terms of binary division have much more complicated relationships to each other than a binary model would allow. For instance a prioritization of kd or Martina's lesbianism over their national, ethnic or racial identity may signify that, however radical the category of the 'masculine lesbian' may be to heterosexuality, the pre-existent whiteness of both lesbianism and heterosexuality underscores this challenge in contemporary western culture. I hope, however, that I have offered a reading here that interrogates the mechanics of identity formation, and the reasons and motives for such exclusions.

In this chapter I have suggested that the heterosexual sex/gender relationship is disturbed by the idealistic representation of lesbian stars. This is achieved through a specific form of lesbian consumption, which involves a rejection of heterosexual imagery – imagery which joins masculine to man and feminine to woman. The lesbian chic figure is a media construction which renders lesbianism palatable for heterosexual consumption, and offers limited opportunity for lesbian identification. However, media images of the lesbian idols Martina and kd, even though they may be read by heterosexuals as mannish, abnormal deviants, invite lesbian identification because they represent an ongoing lesbian identity and culture. As I shall go on to show in the next two chapters, images of kd and Martina provide evidence of a lesbian culture to women who might not have realized that lesbians existed outside of heterosexist folklore – lesbian chic being part of that folklore. As I shall also show, such representations offer the basis from which lesbians may develop strategies for relating to popular culture that further disrupt heterosexist cultural constraints around looking, reading and producing meanings in relation to images and stars.

Notes

1. Judith Butler, 'Imitation and Gender Insubordination' in Diane Fuss (ed.), *Inside/Out: Lesbian Theories, Gay Theories* (London and New York: Routledge, 1991).
2. *Ibid.*, p. 13.
3. Richard Dyer, *Heavenly Bodies: Film Stars and Society* (London: BFI/Macmillan, 1992), p. 159.
4. Victoria Starr, *k.d. lang: All You Get Is Me* (London: HarperCollins, 1994), p. 16.
5. *Ibid.*, p. 23.
6. *Ibid.*, p. 34.
7. Photograph by Tom Braid.
8. See Elizabeth Wilson, 'Deviant Dress', *Feminist Review* 35, Summer 1990, pp. 67–74.
9. Stuart Ewen, *All Consuming Images: The Politics of Style in Contemporary Culture* (London: Basic Books/HarperCollins, 1988), p. 94.
10. *Ibid.*, emphasis in original.

11. *Ibid.*, p. 161.
12. Adrienne Blue, 'The Player', *Guardian (Weekend)*, 19 November 1994, pp. 26–30.
13. See Wilson, 'Deviant Dress'.
14. Gilda Zwerman, *Lives of Notable Gay Men and Lesbians: Martina Navratilova* (New York and Philadelphia: Chelsea House, 1995), p. 91.
15. For an analysis of the butch lesbian sportswoman see Susan K. Cahn, 'From the "Muscle Moll" to the "Butch Ballplayer": Mannishness, Lesbianism, and Homophobia in Women's Sport', *Feminist Studies*, Vol. 19 No. 2, Summer 1993, pp. 342–68.
16. Diana Fuss, *Essentially Speaking: Feminism, Nature and Difference* (London and New York: Routledge, 1989, p. 102.
17. Zwerman, *Martina Navratilova*, pp. 66–7.
18. *Ibid.*, p. 67.
19. *Ibid.*
20. Jackie Stacey, *Star Gazing* (London: Routledge, 1994), p. 153.
21. See Hortense Powdermaker, 'An Anthropologist Looks at the Movies', *The Annals* 254, November 1947, p. 85 (referenced in Ewen, *All Consuming Images*, p. 93).
22. These photographic knowledges are taken from my own experience at art college, where we were versed in the photographic practice of gender stereotyping, which was subsequently passed off as 'artistic representation'.
23. Mim Udovitch, 'k.d. lang', *Rolling Stone* 662, 5 August 1993, pp. 54–7.
24. John Tagg, *The Burden of Representation* (London: Macmillan Education, 1988), p. 8.
25. Robin Marriner, 'Art Practice and Mass Culture: A Reassessment –

Appropriating Pop', *Aspects* 34, 1987, pp. 12–15, (Ludwig Wittgenstein, *Philosophical Investigations* [Oxford: Basil Blackwell, 1988, first published in 1953]).
26. For analyses of race in terms of biological determinism see Kum-Kum Bhavnani, 'Towards a Multicultural Europe? "Race", Nation and Identity, 1992 and Beyond', *Feminist Review* 45, Autumn 1993, pp. 30–45; and Avtar Brah, 'Re-Framing Europe: En-gendered Racisms, Ethnicities and Nationalisms in Contemporary Western Europe', *Feminist Review* 45, Autumn 1993, pp. 9–29.
27. Judith Butler, *Bodies that Matter: On the Discursive Limits of 'Sex'* (London and New York: Routledge, 1993), pp. xi–xii.
28. Sarah Schulman, 'Now a Word from Our Sponsors: The Emergence of a Gay Management Class and It's Impact on the Print Media', a paper given at the University of California at San Diego, 17 January 1994, p. 7.
29. Stacey, *Star Gazing*, p. 206.
30. Ewen, *All Consuming Images*, p. 87.
31. Stacey, *Star Gazing*, p. 206.
32. Blue, 'The Player', p. 26.
33. *Ibid.*
34. *Ibid.*
35. *The Terminator*, directed by James Cameron, 1984.
36. *Robocop*, directed by Paul Verhoeven, 1987.
37. See Michel Foucault, *The History of Sexuality: An Introduction* (London: Peregrine, 1984).
38. Schulman, 'Now a Word from Our Sponsors'.
39. Ewen, *All Consuming Images*, p. 188.
40. *Ibid.*, p. 189, emphasis in original.
41. For an analysis of postmodernist culture see Mike Featherstone, *Consumer Culture and*

Postmodernism (London: Sage, 1993).
42. *Ibid.*, p. 3.
43. *Ibid.*, p. 5.
44. *Ibid.*, p. 6.
45. *Ibid.*, p. 5.
46. *Mojo*, December 1993, p. 66.
47. Leslie Bennets, 'kd lang Cuts it Close', *Vanity Fair*, August 1993, pp. 46–50, 92–6.
48. Bhavnani, 'Towards a Multicultural Europe?', pp. 31–2.
49. Brah, 'Re-framing Europe', p. 11.
50. *Ibid.*, p. 14.
51. *Ibid.*
52. Frederik Barth, 'Introduction' in Frederik Barth (ed.), *Ethnic Groups and Boundaries: The Social Organization of Culture Difference* (London: Allen and Unwin, 1969), pp. 9–38.
53. Brah, 'Re-framing Europe', p. 15.
54. *Ibid.*
55. p. 39.
56. Butler, 'Imitation and Gender Insubordination', p. 19.
57. Butler, *Bodies That Matter*; Richard Dyer, 'White', *Screen*, Vol. 29 No. 4, Autumn 1988, pp. 44–64.
58. Bhavnani, 'Towards a Multicultural Europe?', p. 33.
59. Dyer, 'White', p. 63.
60. Diane Hamer 'Netting the Press: Playing with Martina' in Belinda Budge and Diane Hamer (eds), *The Good, the Bad and the Gorgeous: Popular Culture's Romance with Lesbianism* (London and San Francisco: Pandora, 1994), pp. 57–77.
61. Dyer, *Heavenly Bodies*, p. 43.
62. Dyer, 'White', p. 63.
63. Udovitch, 'k.d. lang', p. 56.
64. Glyn Brown, 'Language of Love', an interview with kd lang, *Ikon*, November 1995, pp. 26–9.
65. Bennets, 'kd lang Cuts it Close', p. 50.
66. Starr, *All You Get Is Me*, p. 3.
67. *Salmonberries*, directed by Percy Adlon, 1991.
68. Louise Allen, 'Salmonberries: Consuming kd lang' in Tamsin Wilton (ed.), *Immortal Invisible: Lesbians and the Moving Image* (London and New York: Routledge, 1995), pp. 70–84.
69. Stacey, *Star Gazing*, p. 126.
70. Matt Snow, 'k.d. Sings the Blues', *Q*, April 1993, pp. 68–74.
71. *Ibid.*, p. 68.

4

Lesbian Fetishism: Fact or Phallacy?

Introduction

In the previous chapter I investigated how identities are often produced
and sustained through the relationship between the consumption practices
of lesbians, and photographic imagery of lesbian idols, in a western society
which is overflowing with visual imagery. I also argued that, because images
of kd and Martina circulate in the mainstream media, this publicizing and
popularization of lesbian identity may prove challenging to heterosexist
structures of gender and sex in contemporary western culture.

In this chapter I want to extend my argument about the importance of
consumption practices in order to examine the popular idea of lesbian
fetishism – a feature of both lesbian academia and lesbian representation.
I want to discuss the idea in much lesbian theory[1] that fetishistic practices
by lesbians are disruptive of heterosexual hegemony and how lesbian fans
of kd and Martina respond to images of their idols which may be
considered 'fetishistic'. My question in this chapter is this: how can we
understand the notion of fetishism in relation to both lesbian-specific
consumption practices and in the ways in which the lesbian may indeed
be constructed, for example through lesbian chic, as a fetish figure in a
homophobic and heterosexually-dominated society?

Meanings of Fetishism

Commodity Fetishism

Karl Marx used the concept of 'commodity fetishism' in *Capital*,[2] where
he argued that in a capitalist society the relationships between people
who produce commodities for each other is really a relationship between
things. Marx notes that there is something 'queer', 'mysterious' and
'enigmatical' about this relationship[3] and that it has come about because
'the relation of the producers to the sum total of their own labour is

presented to them as a social relation, existing not between themselves, but between the products of their labour'.[4] Thus, Marx calls fetishism the phenomenon of the existence of things as commodities, and the fact that the *value* of these commodities in relation to each other bears no relation to their physical properties. Value, he suggests, 'converts every product into a social hieroglyphic'.[5]

The notion of fetishism in Marx's analysis describes how articles with use-value become commodities by virtue of being the products of the labour of individuals or groups who work independently of each other. Therefore, the social character of each producer's labour is created through the acts of exchange that demarcate a capitalist society. This kind of social living means that use-value and exchange-value (which is value *per se* to Marx) become indistinguishable, to the degree that use-value does not exist without exchange-value. Here, commodity fetishism simply means the ability of a commodity to have value (exchange-value) in and of itself, and in relation to other commodities.

Psychoanalytic Fetishism

The psychoanalytic meaning of fetishism appears in Freud's 1927 article 'Fetishism',[6] in which he argues that the fetish is a 'penis-substitute'. He stresses how the little boy (girls are not included) is horror-struck to find the mother has not got a penis; the boy subsequently disavows this absence and the sight of this absence until later in life. When the earlier scene is recalled, so is an object (hair, slipper, lace, shoe) that was originally near the seemingly mutilated female genitals and on which the boys eyes accidentally fell at the time. This object becomes the fetish, and its role is to enable the boy to cope with castration anxiety. When the fetish is seen and desired the mutilated woman is restored to an imaginary wholeness.

In 'Lesbian Fetishism?' Elizabeth Grosz clarifies the meaning of fetishism in both Freudian and Lacanian terms. She argues that, in Freud, a fetish is an object external to the body, or part of the body which symbolizes the mother's lack of a penis. Thus the fetish idea refers to a contradictory position whereby the fetishist, always male, takes another object to represent the mother's missing penis, because he is 'unable to resolve the Oedipal conflict', and 'unable or unwilling to take up the prescribed heterosexual path by abandoning the mother as love-object and accepting the post-Oedipal restraints on his sexual impulses through identification with the authority of the (symbolic) father ...'.[7] She explains that the only way in which women may then become tolerable to the fetishist as sex objects is by substituting a symbolic phallus for the mother's missing one and as a '"token of triumph over the threat of castration and a protection against it"'.[8]

Lacan's theory of the symbolic fundamentally revolves around the 'phallic signifier'. This phallocentric theory relegates women to the imaginary as pre-symbolic, and Lacan equates the feminine with *lack*; hence, women are seen as objects of fetishism, but never subjects of fetishism or desire. Grosz examines Lacan's theory of fetishism, which rests on the notion of the symbolic. She highlights that, in Lacanian theory, the penis as a *phallus* is symbolic:

> There is no symbolic equation between the fetish and the penis because, as Lacan so cogently argues, the phallus is not the equivalent of the penis. ... The relation between phallus and fetish is already entirely bound up with the order of signifiers. The penis (the real organ) can only take on the role of the phallus because it is *missing*, i.e., because women are castrated. The two terms confirmed and denied as equivalent are both signifiers: at no point does the (Lacanian) Real enter the equation.[9]

She goes on to suggest: 'The fetish ... only functions as a sign by virtue of its reference to the phallus, not the penis.'[10]

In this article Grosz questions the relevance of Freud's theory of fetishism in thinking about lesbian fetishism, and uses Lacan's theory of the symbolic in order to try and explore Freud's analysis. In the end she remains ambivalent about the usefulness of Freud's notion of fetishism. The connection Grosz does draw out between lesbianism and Freud's understanding of female fetishism refers to the object of desire that is fetishized by the lesbian. Grosz argues that this object of desire in the lesbian scenario is in fact a 'subject' – another women – stating that the lesbian, 'through this love-object, is able to function as if she *has*, rather than *is*, the phallus'.[11] This point has similarities with de Lauretis's argument in *The Practice of Love*, which I examined in Chapter Two, and which I will explore again later in this chapter.

Grosz initially suggests that the symbolic distance of the phallus from the ontological penis opens up space for such a discussion. However, Judith Butler contests that Lacan implicitly connects the phallus to the penis through the discourse of the symbolic:

If the phallus *must* negate the penis in order to symbolize and signify in its privileged way, then the phallus is bound to the penis, not through simple identity, but through determinate negation. If the phallus only signifies to the extent that it is *not* the penis, and the penis is qualified as that body part that it must *not be*, then the phallus is fundamentally dependant upon the penis in order to symbolize at all. Indeed, the phallus would be nothing without the penis.[12]

In psychoanalysis, therefore, female fetishism is consistently disavowed, and is a strategy for the transposition of desire which is carefully restricted to men, or contained within a framework of male privilege.

In her article 'The Return of Female Fetishism and the Fiction of the Phallus' Anne McClintock challenges a psychoanalytic definition of fetishism. She argues that both Freud's and Lacan's theories involve a phallocentrism which supports the primal unity of the male subject and which denies female agency. McClintock contends that the fetish idea is instrumental in the construction of female desire as a negativity or lack, cleverly maintaining: 'Freud does not explain why the fetish object must be read as a substitute for the mother's (absent) penis, and not, say, as a substitute for the father's (absent) breasts.'[13] McClintock therefore believes that in theorizing female fetishism we must reject the foundational importance of psychoanalytic meaning:

> The concept of telos is nowhere more marked than in Lacan's attempts to disavow female fetishism. Just as Freud could not allow clitoral sexuality to exist beyond puberty (for then female sexuality would escape the telos of heterosexual reproduction and the primacy of male genital pleasure), so too Lacan cannot permit female fetishism to exist. 'Since it has been effectively demonstrated' he proclaims, 'that the imaginary motive for most male perversions is the desire to preserve the phallus which involved the subject in the mother' and since fetishism is the 'virtually manifest case of this desire', fetishism *must* be absent in women.[14]

McClintock subsequently examines how Lacan admits lesbians into fetishism as 'pretend' men:

> with a turn of the page Lacan is forced to admit that fetishism isn't absent in women, but he tries to salvage the phallic drama in two ways. First, he identifies female fetishism only with lesbians. Second, in a

deeply homophobic gesture, Lacan defines lesbians as 'disappointed' heterosexuals. 'Feminine homosexuality', Lacan announces grandly, 'follows from a disappointment which reinforces the side of the demand for love.' But the very concept of 'disappointment' in Lacan, like the concept of 'arrest' in Freud, has meaning only in relation to a prior belief in the normative telos of heterosexual desire, in which one is first 'disappointed', and then turns to lesbianism. Lacan's use of 'perversion' ('to turn away from') itself implies a normative heterosexual development from which the female subject turns, veering in 'disappointment' to the 'mask' and 'virile display' of lesbian desire.[15]

The pre-psychoanalytic history of the word 'fetish' illustrates how a particular view of fetishism relating to cultural icons was in existence before psychoanalysts earmarked the term and restricted its meaning to the arena of sexual desire. As McClintock points out: 'the western discourse on the fetish was at least four centuries old before the phallus was singled out as its central principle'.[16]

The Lesbian as a Fetish-Figure

Danae Clark's article 'Commodity Lesbianism' aptly illustrates how lesbianism is constructed as a fetish in a heterosexually dominated culture. Clark concentrates on how lesbians are both commodified and targeted as a consumer group in the USA. In her analysis she suggests that 'lipstick lesbians' are being hailed by advertisers as consumers, and suggests that new attitudes of openness towards fashion, sexuality and lifestyle may be the result of two factors – the impact of the lesbian-feminist movement and the increased earnings of lesbians:

> According to a recent survey in OUT/LOOK, a national gay and lesbian quarterly, the average annual income for individual lesbians (who read OUT/LOOK) is $30,181; the average lesbian house-hold income is approximately $58,000. Since lesbians as a group are beginning to raise their incomes and class standing, they are now in a position to afford more of the clothing and 'body maintenance' that was once beyond their financial capabilities.[17]

Clark goes on to note that whilst advertisers may be tapping in to a lesbian market, they are also still appealing to heterosexual consumers by using fashion models who look like lesbians:

In one photograph the handsome, short-haired model leans against the handlebars of a motorcycle, an icon associated with bike dyke culture. Her man-styled jacket, tie, and jewelry suggest a butch lesbian style that offers additional points of purchase for the lesbian spectator. ... Lesbian readers ... know that they are not the primary audience for mainstream advertising, that androgyny is a fashionable and profitable commodity, and that the fashion models in these ads are quite probably heterosexual.[18]

Thus the lesbian has become a fetish-figure for the pleasure of heterosexual consumption, merely a highly superficial image, signifying a depthless non-person. Clark sees two sides to this advertising strategy:

media and advertising texts can be analyzed in terms of their (un)willingness or (in)ability to represent the identity politics of current lesbian communities. Gay window advertising ... consciously disavows any explicit connection to lesbianism for fear of offending or losing potential customers. At the same time, an appropriation of lesbian styles or appeal to lesbian desires can also assure a lesbian market. ... Style as resistance becomes commodifiable as chic when it leaves the political realm and enters the fashion world.[19]

The lesbian image as a consumer-sign that Clark investigates here re-demonizes the lesbian as a non-person, an un-subject through commodity fetishism. As Clark concludes: 'gay window advertising appropriates lesbian subcultural style, incorporates its features into commodified representations, and offers it back to lesbian consumers in a packaged form cleansed of identity politics'.[20] However, I would go further than Clark and say that the lesbian consumer is a ruse of contemporary capitalist society, and that the supposed rise in income for lesbians in the USA or Britain is premised on highly debatable statistics.[21]

In *Shopping with Freud*, Rachel Bowlby discusses the interconnection between psychoanalytic knowledges and consumer culture in the west. In the first paragraph of her book she clarifies her position:

By the 1930s, it is feasible to imagine a partnership to the point of identification between on the one hand a psychology typified by psychoanalysis and on the other the mass consumption and production suggested by the car; and the association is appropriately encapsulated by one of the verbal techniques of modern publicity, the sloganising style of a near homonym. The Ford-Freud doubling suggests that consumption and psychology together made or will make the late-modern world: that for all practical purposes (and there are no others) they are one.[22]

In her book Bowlby offers a series of case studies. She reads texts such as D. H. Lawrence's *Lady Chatterley's Lover*, Mary Shelley's *Frankenstein* and the case of 'Anna "O"' in the writings of Freud and Breuer. In all of these studies she constructs comparisons and interconnections between the prevalence of psychoanalysis in the development of the 'subject' and the 'subject' as a 'consumer' in twentieth-century society. The subject, she argues, is at the centre of consumerist logic; the subject has a psychology which salespeople attempt to tap in to in order to sell products to consumers. Bowlby deconstructs the texts that she references in relation both to this phenomenon of the consuming subject and the changes in society and culture against which this notion of the subject has developed.

The interconnection of the psychoanalytic notion of desire with commodification has also been noticed by Grosz, in her article 'Refiguring Lesbian Desire':

this notion of desire as an absence, lack, or hole, an abyss seeking to be engulfed, stuffed to satisfaction, is ... uniquely useful in capitalist models of acquisition, propriety, and ownership (seeing the object of desire on the model of the consumable commodity) ...[23]

The argument about the interconnection of psychoanalysis and consumerism is important in relation to the idea of the lesbian consumer. The question of the lesbian consumer is a difficult one. I do not believe that the lesbian consumer is produced by dominant advertising ideologies which promote lesbian styles and deny a lived-out lesbian identity (a consumer of this kind is a media construction). Nevertheless, I do believe in a lesbian consumer who sees, reads, consumes and desires cultural products which open up spaces for thinking of lesbianism as a lived-out identity.

The representations of kd and Martina that I have analysed in this book so far provide such spaces, though in some the space for interpretation by lesbians is limited and often fraught with homophobic insignia. I will attempt to analyse such 'controversial' images in relation both to their production in a homophobic society which fetishizes the lesbian and in relation to the responses to them by the lesbian fans of kd and Martina.

kd lang and the Missing Penis

She has seen it and knows that she is without it and wants to have it.[24]

Psychoanalytic theory is repeatedly referenced in popular culture. This referencing is particularly significant when it takes place in relation to lesbian sexuality, as, often, psychoanalytic discourse is used to deride and demonize masculine lesbians in and through dominant cultural exchanges. The assertion that lesbians want to 'be' men is typical of the construction of the masculine lesbian as deviant, and the psychoanalytic idea of 'penis envy' is often used to secure this derisory construction.

The photographs of kd lang in the August 1993 issue of *Vanity Fair* that I have mentioned in previous chapters clearly reference this construction of 'the lesbian who wants to be a man'. In this chapter I want to discuss the cover image of the magazine, which depicts kd lang being shaved by Cindy Crawford, and also a sepia-toned image from inside the magazine, which shows a side view of kd's face licking a small mirror that she is holding. Both images have acquired an iconic value in lesbian culture. Bearing in mind this value in both lesbian and mainstream culture, how can we understand the images in terms which suggest a resistance to this derisory idea of the lesbian with penis envy?

The notion of penis envy was developed by Freud in order to account for one way in which women may disavow castration. In this first extract from his 1917 essay 'On Transformations of Instinct as Exemplified in Anal Eroticism', Freud argues that in the development of the libido 'genital primacy' must be preceded by anal eroticism. He concludes that in relation to 'ideas', 'phantasies' and 'symptoms' in the unconscious, the concepts of '*faeces ... baby* and *penis* are ill-distinguished from one another and are easily interchangeable'.[25] For an example, he includes this description of penis envy in the woman:

> If we penetrate deeply enough into the neurosis of a woman, we not infrequently meet with the repressed wish to possess a penis like a man. We call this wish 'envy for a penis' and include it in the castration complex. Chance mishaps in the life of such a woman, mishaps which are themselves frequently the result of a very masculine disposition,

have re-activated this infantile wish and, through the backward flow of libido, made it the chief vehicle of her neurotic symptoms. In other women we find no evidence of this wish for a penis; it is replaced by a wish for a baby, the frustration of which in real life can lead to the outbreak of a neurosis.[26]

In a later essay, which he wrote in 1925, entitled 'Some Psychical Consequences of the Anatomical Distinction Between the Sexes', Freud discusses the various routes for women out of the Oedipus complex. He suggests that the woman develops what he terms 'the masculinity complex' in order to disavow her own castration, or as a way of explaining to herself her 'lack of a penis':[27]

The hope of some day obtaining a penis in spite of everything and so of becoming like a man may persist to an incredibly late age and may become a motive for strange and otherwise unaccountable actions. Or again, a process may set in which I should like to call a 'disavowal', a process which in the mental life of children seems neither uncommon nor very dangerous but which in an adult would mean the beginning of a psychosis. Thus a girl may refuse to accept the fact of being castrated, may harden herself in the conviction that she does possess a penis, and may subsequently be compelled to behave as though she were a man.[28]

The *Vanity Fair* cover image representing scantily dressed Cindy Crawford shaving kd lang must rank as one of the most controversial contemporary images of lesbianism, in terms of the way it draws on Freud's discourse of penis envy and the notion that lesbians are either 'pretend men' or 'want to be men'. In the photograph kd wears a pinstriped 'man's' suit and leans back in a barber's chair, whilst Cindy cavorts playfully behind her in high heels and adopting a classically pornographic pose, with her bare legs wide apart and her head flung back and to the side. The stark white background is also reminiscent of the bright lighting often used in pornographic photography.

Appearing on the cover of *Vanity Fair*, a glossy, high-status international lifestyle magazine, the image reached a vast audience and has certainly brought lesbian chic to mainstream attention. Here kd's status as a lesbian icon is fetishized because she is pictured with Cindy who, although rumours have abounded about her supposed bisexuality, has been married to Richard Gere and is thus *not* a lesbian. Furthermore, the fetish is twofold: kd is a fetish for Cindy's playful desire, and the image itself is a fetishistic scenario of heterosexual male pornographic fantasy, in which two ladies languish lustfully together.

Having said that, however, this image does depict a lesbian who clearly lives out her identity. Whatever Cindy's sexuality may be, kd *identifies* as a lesbian. The consumption of this picture by fans of kd, then, is important for interrogating what kinds of discourses the image engages with. Many of kd's fans did not like the image: June describes how she and other kd fans discussed the photograph during one of their 'kd nights':

> I don't know if you saw the *Vanity Fair* article on kd earlier this year (August, I think). I think that caused the most major hiccup in kd circles, certainly amongst the people I know, and certainly in me. I'd rung up the hotline and it was kd herself on the answering machine (this is always very exciting when she does that, it's like you've rung her up for a chat, oh dear, anyway ...) and she was going on about how wonderful the pictures in it were, so when I actually saw them I was quite shocked to say the least. I know several people who don't even like her anymore because of it. I felt angry when I saw it, I couldn't work out why she'd want to pose like that, it felt like a very male almost *Playboy* sort of thing to do. I felt like maybe I was supposed to feel it was OK because it was two women. Since then I've met people who thought it was good (they were all American) and I wondered if maybe I was just overreacting in a sort of prudish way. I don't know really, I still don't like it, I don't think it's necessary, I think it's what Cindy Crawford was wearing that was the worst thing. I don't think it's as bad as I did, I suppose. I've got used to it, but I still wonder why she did it.

It seems that June's shock at the *Vanity Fair* image is, at least in part, related to her national identity. When she points out that all the lesbians she spoke to who liked the image were American, she makes a crucial distinction that relates to how she sees herself as a British lesbian. The difference between British and American popular culture is evident here, when she questions if her reaction was 'prudish'. An over-commodification of lesbianism in the American press is perhaps one reason why this image of kd is unacceptable to her. However, whilst the commodification of lesbianism is certainly an issue for me in this book, the problem lies with the forms of domination expressed and reproduced through such commodification, and not with commodification *per se*; derisory stereotypes of masculine lesbians are certainly abundant in the British press.

This next quote from Freda illustrates how 'lesbian chic' images such as the *Vanity Fair* cover represent lesbianism as a fetish – as a commodity for commodity's sake. Significantly, Freda mistakes Cindy Crawford for Madonna, and *Vanity Fair* for *Vogue*, a testimony to the abundance of superficial images of lesbian chic in the mainstream press:

> I don't think that she is perfect. When that picture was printed on the cover of *Vogue* (was it?) with her being shaved by Madonna, I was put off. She was under the pretence of being a man, and this I think is the wrong press for lesbians to get. Too many people stereotype lesbians as trying to be men, when what I think a lesbian is, is a woman loving a woman, and being happy and comfortable with that. I don't think that kd lang should have backed up that image, being one of the few famous lesbians.
>
> *(Freda)*

The point I am making here is that, through the vehicle of popular iconic lesbian chic imagery, 'the lesbian' is being represented as a fetish-figure, a fetish for male pornographic fantasies. However, this does not mean that lesbian fans of kd do not, or indeed should not, take pleasure in looking at the images in *Vanity Fair*. As these next quotes illustrate, many fans liked the images. In this first extract Estelle takes pleasure from the image and reveals how it was an important point of identification in her own 'coming out':

> I really love kd. She definitely is to me what you could call an 'idol'. I do everything I can to look like she does in the *Vanity Fair* picture where's she is being shaved by Cindy Crawford (my most prized possession is the *VF* mag!). I bought a man's suit (my first!), and had my hair cut to match hers!

This identification with kd undercuts the fetishistic connotations of the image: because Estelle wants to live out a lesbian identity just like kd, the superficiality of the lesbian chic figure as a fetish – as just a sign – is disrupted.

In contrast, Sal identifies with the position of Cindy Crawford in the photo-shoot. However, her reading also disrupts the notion of the lesbian as a fetish, because, in a fantasy scenario, Sal substitutes herself, a 'real' lesbian, in the place of Cindy. This effectively disrupts the homophobic idea of lesbianism as a commodity fetish-figure as, for Sal, Cindy is not lesbian enough, because Cindy does not *identify* as a lesbian:

> I was elated when I saw kd on the cover of *Vanity Fair* with Cindy Crawford. I loved the contrast of kd's butchness and Cindy's femme image. I had the front cover on my bedroom wall for about two years. I was so glad that kd wasn't trying to look acceptably feminine for the mostly heterosexual readership of *Vanity Fair*. She was so sexy in a man's suit. I thought Cindy was so lucky to be able to dress up skimpily and seduce her! I used to fantasize about being Cindy during the photo-shoot. We would be told by the photo director to pretend to kiss, as they did. But kd wouldn't be able to resist stroking my long luscious hair, or kissing my perfectly lipsticked lips (not at all how I look in real life!). We would roll around on the floor, messing up the set. The director and camera crew would be laughing and shouting at us to stop, but we'd be so passionately delirious we wouldn't care. We'd stay together for ever. I'd be the perfect 'wife' for kd, and all her fans would be jealous of me.

Whether or not kd's fans *like* the images in *Vanity Fair*, it seems that the lesbian as a faceless and superficial fetish-figure is being undermined by lesbian identification practices.

The other image in *Vanity Fair* that I want to look at more closely references Freud's idea of penis envy. The interview even quotes a reference by lang to Freud's concept. It reads: 'I have a little bit of penis envy, they're ridiculous but they're cool.' In this picture kd cradles a small purse-size mirror in her hand, the sort of mirror that is normally used for the kind of feminine display associated with the application of make-up and the plucking of facial hair; indeed, her eyebrows are plucked in a sharp line and her lips seem painted, details that are characteristic of a typically western femininity. In contrast to this reference to femininity kd's hand is laden with large chunky rings typically associated with masculinity.

kd's head occupies the rest of the image; her eyes, almost closed, seductively gaze down in the direction of her open mouth and her tongue, the tip of which barely touches the surface of the mirror. All we can see reflected is the tip of her tongue: tongue-tip touching tongue-tip. The centrality of the tongue in this image, combined with the quote about penis-envy that accompanies the picture, suggests that we read kd's tongue as a penis substitute – as a fetish in psychoanalytic terms.

The mirror is also significant in this context of lesbian fetishism. In Lacanian theory the (mis)recognition of one's reflection as a unified and ideal self marks the critical moment in the protracted process through which the subject is both split and constituted. For Lacan the acquisition of language represents the symbolic entry into culture, but the subject is consistently threatened with a fragmentation that is structured by absence. In *Feminine Sexuality* Jacqueline Rose outlines Lacan's argument that Freud's developmental concepts rest on the myth of a subjective cohesion that the unconscious subverts, and how he felt that Freud's most fundamental discovery was 'that the unconscious never ceases to challenge our apparent identity as subjects'.[29]

It is through this disturbing status of the unconscious that Lacan insists we must understand the 'mirror stage', as Rose maintains:

> in the 1930s he introduced the concept of the 'mirror stage' … which took the child's mirror image as the model and basis for its future identifications. This image is a fiction because it conceals, or freezes, the infant's lack of motor co-ordination and the fragmentation of its drives. But it is salutary for the child, since it gives it the first sense of a coherent identity in which it can recognise itself. For Lacan, however, this is already a fantasy – the very image which places the child divides its identity into two. Furthermore, that moment only has meaning in relation to the presence and the look of the mother who guarantees its reality for the child. The mother does not … mirror the child to itself; she grants an image *to* the child, which her presence instantly deflects. Holding the child is, therefore, to be understood not only as a containing, but as a process of referring, which fractures the unity it seems to offer. The mirror image is central to Lacan's account of subjectivity, because its apparent smoothness and totality is a myth. The image in which we first recognise ourselves is a *mis-recognition*.[30]

The mirror in the image of kd in the pages of *Vanity Fair* may be read as a fetish for the lesbian's prohibited entry into culture or the lesbian's position as an unsubject.[31] The centrality of the mirror in this image is suggestive of Lacan's proposition that all subjectivity is structured by absence. However, if we understand psychoanalysis to have a heterosexist underpinning, this proposition could conversely signify that heterosexual subjectivity is whole and complete, and that, by contrast, lesbian subjectivity is not. Thus, Lacanian theory is problematic to an understanding of lesbian identity and culture, because it is heterosexist; but problems also arise in relation to an understanding of contemporary western culture, where we are faced with heterosexual constructions of lesbianism as a non-identity, as purely a sign, a lesbian chic fetish-figure. In other words, the argument Lacan puts forward to assert that *all* identity is structured by absence ignores the material subordination of lesbians through heterosexuality's regime of wholeness and fixity.

Understanding kd as a lesbian star, however, allows for a reading of the *Vanity Fair* images that goes 'against the grain' of homophobic psychoanalytic discourse. The gender contradictions in the mirror photograph, between kd's masculine suit and jewellery and her use of feminine items and characteristics set the scene for a reading of this image which may resist a complete submersion of lesbianism within the psychoanalytic discourse of fetishism and the idea that lesbians 'want to be men'. Here, 'the lesbian' is certainly represented as a commodity-fetish, an object of pure exchange-value in heterosexual culture, but this is not just an image of a lesbian, this is an image of kd lang, a lesbian icon who lives out her lesbian identity, and in so doing resists the articulation of a lesbian chic fetish-figure dependent on giving pleasure to a heterosexual readership. This next quote from a kd fan emphasizes how the lesbian consumption of kd is, generally, through a resistance to lesbian chic:

> Pride did a lot for me. I did accept to myself as well as others that I was gay, but more importantly fate threw me at my girlfriend, Lenora, who I love very much. She too is a kd fan, but from a lot further back and according to her I'm definitely obsessed. kd made me question a lot of my conceptions of who I liked and the more I think about it now the more I realise that my stumbling across her ... was an important and crucial turning point for me. I believe I'm lucky to have found this before the present hype of being lesbian caught up with her, or me, otherwise I honestly believe that I would have argued over my motives behind what I thought I felt.

> *(Zoe)*

The lesbian fans in my study see the authenticity of kd's lesbian identity as overriding the more superficial and impermanent sign-value of lesbian chic. For Zoe, the authenticity of the lesbianism that her idol represented helped her to address her initial tentative feelings about becoming a lesbian – a decision which would have been more difficult had she come out since the increased popularization of lesbian chic as a commodity-fetish.

However, just as lesbian chic as a commodity for heterosexual pleasures is being rejected by lesbian fans of kd and Martina, theorists concerned with lesbian identity are favouring an approach which underscores the fetishistic practices of lesbians as resistant to heterosexual oppression. De Lauretis's analysis of lesbian desire in *The Practice of Love*[32] centres on the erotic and genital relations between women, and is an examination of lesbian fetishism. She refuses a traditional psychoanalytic model that views female sexual desire as active only in relation to the masculinity complex and penis envy, and yet she links lesbian desire to the structure of fetishism. In order to establish this link, her theory of fetishism turns on the castration complex and the notion of 'disavowal'.

Briefly to recap, in Freudian theory lesbian desire is figured in terms of the 'masculinity complex', which is the result of an unresolved Oedipus complex in the lesbian as a girl – a kind of 'faulty' development. In this 'faulty' scenario the girl disavows her own castrated condition and retains a masculine and active identity, rather than reluctantly accepting her own lack of the phallus and desiring those who 'have' it – namely men.

De Lauretis's aim is to move beyond the masculinity complex, in order to see perverse desire via a notion of disavowal and not repression. Thus she replaces Freud's fetish object of body *part* with the *entire* female body, arguing that it is not the absence of a penis on her own body that the *girl* disavows (as in Freud), but, rather, it is the absence of another (her mother's, or even her own) woman's body that the *woman* disavows and must displace on to a fetish substitute. As I explained in Chapter Two de Lauretis reinscribes the notion of castration through a reference to the character of Stephen Gordon in Radclyffe Hall's *The Well of Loneliness*,[33] and describes the types of lesbian cultural practices which may constitute forms of lesbian fetishism:

> what the lesbian desires in a woman ... is indeed not a penis but a part or perhaps the whole of the female body, or something metonymically related to it, such as physical, intellectual, or emotional attributes,

stance, attitudes, appearance, self-presentation – and hence the importance of clothing, costume, performance, etc. in lesbian subcultures ...[34]

McClintock also cites several examples of female fetishism; however, unlike de Lauretis, McClintock believes such practices exceed a psychoanalytic model. She suggests that the 'female fetish scene flourishes' in the cultural practices of wearing 'high heels and hot lingerie, lipstick and leather', 'dildos and suspenders', and experiencing 'bondage and discipline', 'food and fantasy, chocolates and perfume'.[35] She also refers to lesbian cross-dressing as a form of fetishism:

> In Manhattan, Diane Torr (alias Hamish McAllister), sprightly in a sporran and moustache, hosts a cross-dressers' evening of bawdy bagpipes and poetry. At Torr's cross-dressing workshop for women, we bandage our breasts, don moustaches and mannish clothes, and then, schooled in the conventions of male street-space and toilet etiquette, sally into the night to savour gender ambiguity.[36]

Using such examples of often lesbian-specific social practices McClintock argues for a theoretical move to understand the place of psychoanalytic discourse in the lives of women. In her concluding comments she suggests that 'fetishism might become the theoretical scene of a renewed investigation into the vexed relations between psychoanalysis and social history – if only because the fetish itself embodies the failure of a single narrative of origins'.[37] McClintock's article is important because she suggests possibilities for theorizing about lesbian fetishism and desire which do not rely on a psychoanalytic framework rife with structures of binary difference, male privilege and heterosexism.

De Lauretis and McClintock's descriptions of specific lesbian fetishes provide one way to read the pictures of kd in *Vanity Fair*. Nevertheless, de Lauretis's discussion of fetishism in relation to lesbianism is problematic, as her analysis fails to account for how lesbianism itself is fetishized in heterosexual culture through lesbian chic. McClintock's analysis, by contrast, suggests that we should start to examine the relationship between psychoanalysis and social history – a position similar to my own. Encouraging the highlighting of ways in which the lesbian is fetishized in contemporary capitalist society, and how heterosexual domination is achieved through this strategy, such an analysis also examines how resistances to this fetishistic construction are articulated through the lesbian star/fan relationship.

Martina's Penetrating Forehand

The consumption of psychoanalytic knowledge is important to my reading of the two photographs of Martina's hands and arms that I discussed in the previous chapter. I examined these images in relation to ideas of fragmentation and muscularity, and using Stacey's argument[38] about how the fragmentation of the female body by female consumers contributes to pleasurable viewing experiences and identifications, I suggested that the consumption of Martina as a lesbian idol through such representations is important to the construction of lesbian identities at a wider level.

I want now to extend the analysis of these photographs to an understanding of how fetishistic desire amongst lesbians may be produced in the acts of consumption of both the photographs themselves and the subject matter of Martina's muscular arms and hands. In both these photographs these famous lesbian hands reference the male attributes of action, prowess, strength, triumph, dedication and, importantly, *agency*. The *Curve* cover image reflects Martina's status as an object of desire in lesbian culture. Her tightly clenched fist and muscular forearm hold the viewer in the centre of the image. The pose is a classic one in sport – the player, on winning a point or a match shouts and holds a victorious arm up to the crowd.

The other photograph, which I have chosen for the cover of *The Lesbian Idol* because of its iconic value in lesbian culture, can also be read in terms of fetishism. This long image vertically follows the central line of Martina's arm, which is stretched upward as she prepares to serve; the bottom of the picture is the base of her arm, with her head behind it, and the short sleeve of her T-shirt is pulled tightly against the upward arm movement. A small gap between the top edge of the image and the tip of Martina's middle finger recalls the erotic positioning of 'not-quite touching' that so often tantalizes audiences of romantic films. The ball is not in the frame of the picture and her splayed empty fingers, replete with heavy jewellery, express a desire to grasp the ball that hovers out of shot, but also evoke a victory gesture. Martina squints upward through her glasses and her mouth is open enough for her teeth to be visible. The sheer determination on her face and the upward stretch of her muscular and heavily veined arm and hand reflect the desire for success. These photographs, taken during the 1994 Wimbledon tennis championships, were shot at the height of Martina's fame as a lesbian icon but also at the end of her outstanding career. In both of these images the hands are instantly recognizable as Martina's, and they draw on knowledges about Martina that circulate amongst lesbians worldwide.

How may Martina's arms be read as phallic in these two photographs? The sexual connotation of the muscular male body suggests physicality and sexuality. The sexual connotations here are specific to lesbian experience, as the arm and hand are fetishized. These images may well be read in terms of oppressive homophobic ideas about penis envy or lesbians wanting to be men. Judith Butler attempts to usurp the patriarchal privilege that the phallus-as-signifier-of-penis enjoys, and questions why it should be *assumed* that the phallus requires the penis in order to signify, and thus wonders why it could not operate through symbolizing other body parts:

> If the phallus operates as a signifier whose privilege is under contest, if its privilege is shown to be secured precisely through the reification of logical and structural relations within the symbolic, then the structures within which it is put into play are more various and revisable that the Lacanian scheme can affirm. Consider that 'having' the phallus can be symbolised by an arm, a tongue, a hand (or two), a knee, a thigh, a pelvic bone, an array of purposefully instrumentalized body-like things.[39]

She also suggests:

> Inasmuch as the phallus signifies, it is also always in the process of being signified. In this sense, it is not the incipient moment or origin of a signifying chain, as Lacan would insist, but part of a reiterable signifying practice and, hence, open to resignification: signifying in ways and in places that exceed its proper structural place within the Lacanian symbolic and contest the necessity of that place. If the phallus is a privileged signifier, it gains that privilege through being reiterated. And if the cultural construction of sexuality compels a repetition of that signifier, there is nevertheless in the very force of repetition, understood as resignification or recirculation, the possibility of deprivileging the signifier.[40]

The images of Martina's arms and hands, however, are produced within a homophobic western culture, within which, as I have argued, lesbians are constructed through fetishism by a heterosexually dominated media. By using Butler's theory of the 'lesbian phallus' are we not articulating lesbian identity in the language of the dominant? Exactly how can it be deconstructive of heterosexual oppression to discuss Martina's arm or hand as a phallus when we are surrounded by images of lesbian chic as a fetish-figure? If we examine how Martina's lesbian fans articulate their adoration for their idol, I think we can see a marked difference between lesbian fetishism – the desire for Martina's *arm* (a practice which would lend itself to Butler's theory of the 'lesbian phallus') – and lesbian desire – the desire for *Martina*. This quote from Sadie highlights how desire for Martina enables her to construct her lesbian identity through an identification with her idol:

> I think she is really, really sexy. I don't usually go for the butch type, but being butch myself (so people have told me!) I suppose I identified with her. But it's funny because I always thought I fancied her more than I wanted to *be* her, or be like her. Her muscles are outrageously gorgeous, her physique is so beautiful, her legs are so sexy and strong and her arms and hands are just so muscular and gorgeous. Every inch of her body is wonderful and sexy: I suppose she has the perfect lesbian body, although I know many lesbians would probably disagree because it's not that fashionable to be masculine or butch these days – you've only got to see Beth in *Brookside* to understand that. We get to see a lot of her body on TV in tennis matches ... so much gorgeous Martina to drool over. I'd always watch her and study every part of her body really carefully when she was on TV. I'd watch her shoulders covered by that sexy T-shirt, and look at where her thighs met the line of her underwear – to me she was so perfect ...

In this next extract Lisa talks of having fantasies about Martina, and underscores how Martina's importance as an object of desire is intertwined with her importance as a strong, powerful and 'out' role model for lesbians of all ages:

> By the mid-1980s she was one of my main 'fantasy life' targets. Not that I still did the knight-in-armour routine. No, more like bumping into her at tennis matches and knocking the rackets out of her hand, picking

them up and going on from there. Always cool, calm, irresistible ... walks on beaches, candlelit dinners, log fires, etc. etc. I always knew what to do, what to say. I also was always the perfect lover, wonderful in bed (as was she) and of course she fell hopelessly in love with me. ... She's strong, graceful. I think of her as a panther – lithe, beautiful, powerful. I think she's sexy, very attractive, sometimes even beautiful; I've seen several 'spreads' of her (mid-1989 springs to mind, hair short and spiky at the front and top, and longer at the back, or more recently in *Gay Times*) when I'd say that was a fair description. As well as being incredibly attracted to her, I admire her, for her honesty, her refusal to be anything other than herself. I was a bit disappointed with her in the early 1980s when she called herself 'bisexual' but she's more than made up for that recently. I'd love to meet her, it's great to have her as a strong woman, especially a gay woman, and to have her at the top, the best ever in her field. She gives young dykes a positive, powerful role model. Come to think of it she gives us late thirties and not so young dykes a powerful role model as well. ... She's certainly my No. 1 pin-up, and also the No. 1 on the list of famous women I would love to have an affair with.

Another highly significant image of Martina appeared in the *Guardian*, (*Weekend*) in 1994[41] at the end of her singles tennis career and illustrates how my reading of particular images of Martina may challenge the relationship of gender to sex. It also shows how such images may be read as a form of satire of popular knowledges about sex and gender. In this photograph Martina is shot in a deliberately posed pin-up style, showing off her muscular right arm and hand in a way that suggests this part of her body has indeed gained a fabled status not just amongst lesbians but perhaps a wider audience as well. Martina's hair is slicked back and her arm may even have been oiled to emphasize the sharp, strong contours of her muscles. She is pictured in a typically masculine pose that is reminiscent of the way in which men often show off their worked-out bodies to admiring females.

The satirical effect of this image is secured by Martina's straight look to camera – proudly exhibiting her muscled limb as if she knows she is desired by lesbian audiences – but also by the diamond ear-stud she wears, which sparkles daringly and contrasts sharply with her pose and the physical masculinity of her well-trained body. The accompanying article is entitled 'The Player',[42] a title that also connotes the 'gender-play' inherent in the contrasting of masculine and feminine cultural codes in the image.

Conclusion

Throughout this chapter I have argued that the essentially homophobic and sexist nature of psychoanalytic theory provides an inadequate model for investigating lesbian identifications and lesbian culture. Overall I am in agreement with Grosz when she states that to rework psychoanalysis, or indeed any male privileging discourse, in terms of lesbian desire is an ultimately fruitless project for lesbian theory. She claims of de Lauretis's *The Practice of Love*:

> Attempts to fit women, or in de Lauretis's case lesbians, into these frameworks is bound to be intellectually profitable – one learns an immense amount about these frameworks, and their limits in the process – but in the long run, they prove impossible.[43]

Although the lesbian chic figure undoubtedly acts as a fetish for heterosexual male consumption and, further, represents the coincidence of psychoanalysis and consumerism, I have suggested that lesbian consumers take pleasure in images of kd and Martina that are immediately meaningful as fetishistic (such as the *Vanity Fair* images) *in spite of* this fetishism. In other words, rather than reading such images through fetishism, lesbian fans override a fetishistic meaning or the discourse of fetishism in order to identify with, or desire, their idols in an authenticating manoeuvre.

Such consumption practices generate a resistance to the media spectacle of lesbian chic, whilst reaffirming a lived-out lesbian identity within a lesbian culture. As I explained in Chapter Three, lesbian fans idolize kd and Martina because they are authentic lesbians. Attempts by the mainstream media to constrain these lesbian stars within the regulating notion of lesbian chic is a damaging project, but at one level it also fails, because lesbian audiences consistently resist this over-simplistic construction, which has emerged from within the discourse of heterosexual male erotic fantasy. Rather, lesbians persist in strategies of identification which show how innovative lesbian culture is at making space for itself against the odds. In the next chapter I will go on to analyse the fans' letters in more depth, examining how their idolization of kd and Martina disrupts both the conventional heterosexual structure of romance and the regulating regime of the gaze.

Notes

1. For analyses of lesbian fetishism as transformative see Della Grace, 'Xenomorphisis', *New Formations: A Journal of Culture/Theory/ Politics, Perversity Issue* No. 19, Spring 1993, pp. 125–30; Parveen Adams, 'The Three (Dis)Graces', *New Formations: A Journal of Culture/Theory/Politics, Perversity Issue*, No. 19, Spring 1993, pp. 131–8 and *The Emptiness of the Image: Psychoanalysis and Sexual Differences* (London and New York: Routledge, 1996); Teresa de Lauretis, *The Practice of Love: Lesbian Sexuality and Perverse Desire* (Bloomington and Indianapolis: Indiana University Press, 1994). Also, for critiques of lesbian fetishism and the use of psychoanalytic theory in debates about lesbianism see Heather Findlay, 'Freud's "Fetishism" and the Lesbian Dildo Debates' in Corey K. Creekmur and Alexander Doty (eds), *Out in Culture: Gay, Lesbian and Queer Essays on Popular Culture* (London: Cassell, 1995), pp. 328–42; Elizabeth Grosz, 'Lesbian Fetishism?', *Differences*, Vol. 3 No. 2, Summer 1991, pp. 39–54; Diane Hamer, 'Significant Others: Lesbianism and Psychoanalytic Theory', *Feminist Review*, No. 34, Spring 1990, pp. 134–51; Melanie Storr, 'Psychoanalysis and Lesbian Desire: The Trouble with Female Homosexuals' in Joe Bristow and Angela R. Wilson (eds), *Activating Theory: Lesbian, Gay, Bisexual Politics* (London: Lawrence and Wishart, 1993), pp. 53–69.

2. Karl Marx, 'The Fetishism of Commodities and the Secret Thereof' (first published in 1867) in Frederick Engels (ed.), *Capital: A Critique of Political Economy, Volume 1, Capitalist Production,* (London: Lawrence and Wishart, 1970) pp. 71–83.

3. *Ibid.*, p. 72.

4. *Ibid.*

5. *Ibid.*, p. 74.

6. Sigmund Freud, 'Fetishism' in *On Sexuality* (London: Pelican Books, 1977, first published in 1927) pp. 345–58.

7. Grosz, 'Lesbian Fetishism?', p. 42.

8. Freud, 'Fetishism', quoted in Grosz, *ibid.*

9. *Ibid.*, p. 43.

10. *Ibid.*, p. 44.

11. *Ibid.*, p. 51, emphasis in original.

12. Judith Butler, *Bodies that Matter: On the Discursive Limits of 'Sex'* (London and New York: Routledge, 1993), p. 84.

13. Anne McClintock, 'The Return of Female Fetishism and the Fiction of the Phallus', *New Formations* 19, 1993, pp. 1–22.

14. *Ibid.*, p. 8, emphasis in original.

15. *Ibid.*

16. *Ibid.*, p. 5.

17. Danae Clark, 'Commodity Lesbianism', *Camera Obscura*, Vol. 25–6, 1991, pp. 180–201.

18. *Ibid.*, pp. 187–8.

19. *Ibid.*, p. 193.

20. *Ibid.*, p. 194.

21. See Sarah Schulman, 'Now a Word from Our Sponsor: The Emergence of a Gay Management Class and Its Impact on the Print Media', a paper given at the University of California at San Diego, 17 January 1994, pp. 1–15.

22. Rachel Bowlby, *Shopping with Freud* (London and New York: Routledge, 1993), p. 1.

23. Elizabeth Grosz, 'Refiguring Lesbian Desire' in Laura Doan (ed.), *The Lesbian Postmodern* (New York: Columbia University Press, 1994), p. 71.

24. Sigmund Freud, 'Some Psychical Consequences of the Anatomical Distinction Between the Sexes' in *On Sexuality* (London, Pelican Books, 1977, first published in 1925), pp. 323–44.

25. Sigmund Freud, 'On Transformations of an Instinct as Exemplified in Anal Eroticism' in *On Sexuality* (London: Pelican Books, 1977, first published in 1917), pp. 293–301, emphasis in original.

26. *Ibid.*, p. 297.

27. Freud, 'Some Physical Consequences', pp. 336–7.

28. Freud, 'Anal Eroticism', p. 337.

29. Juliet Mitchel and Jacqueline Rose (eds), Feminine Sexuality: Jacques Lacan and the École Freudienne (London: Macmillan Press, 1985), p. 30.

30. *Ibid.*

31. See Butler, *Bodies that Matter*, for an analysis of 'abjects'.

32. De Lauretis, *The Practice of Love*.

33. Radclyffe Hall, *The Well of Loneliness* (London: Virago, 1984, first published by Jonathan Cape in 1928).

34. De Lauretis, *The Practice of Love*, p. 228.

35. McClintock, 'The Return of Female Fetishism', p. 1.

36. *Ibid.*

37. *Ibid.*, p. 21.

38. Jackie Stacey, *Star Gazing* (London: Routledge, 1994).

39. Butler, *Bodies that Matter*, p. 88.

40. *Ibid.* p. 89.

41. Cover, the *Guardian (Weekend)*, 19 November 1994, Annie Liebovitz/Contact.

42. This article in the *Guardian* is an extract of a biography of Martina by Adrienne Blue, ('The Player', *Guardian (Weekend)*, 19 November 1994, pp. 26–30).

43. Elizabeth Grosz, 'The Labours of Love, Analysing Perverse Desire: An Interrogation of Teresa de Lauretis's *The Practice of Love*', *Differences*, Vol. 6 Nos 2 and 3, Summer–Autumn 1994, p. 288.

5

Romancing the Masculine:
Lesbian Fans of Lesbian Stars

within two months I had taken this person inside of me body and soul.
I was absolutely intoxicated by everything about her, she could do no
wrong.

(Zoe, a kd fan)

if by some miracle she did find me, and just cocked her little finger at
me and said 'come' – I'd go. Wherever she led. Whatever it cost.
Abandon job, house, the lot. Because there's just no one else like her,
anywhere ...

(Lisa, a Martina fan)

Introduction

In the previous two chapters I suggested that the stardom of kd and
Martina severely troubles heterosexual domination, which is often
cemented through the media, and the discourse of stardom in particular.
In Chapter Three I analysed how this phenomenon of lesbian stardom
disrupts the central focus of heterosexual identifications and desires which
structures the Hollywood-based star system. In Chapter Four I suggested
that particular visual images of kd and Martina may be read fetishistically
as lesbian chic for a heterosexual audience in western consumer culture,
but also how this construction is undercut by the anti-fetishistic readings
of their lesbian fans.

In this chapter I will take this argument about the disruption of
heterosexual domination through lesbian media stardom in a specific
direction, analysing in particular the phenomenon of lesbian fandom.
The extracts above testify to the extreme adoration felt by lesbian fans
towards lesbian stars. I will therefore examine how this fandom may

challenge not only the reproduction of heterosexuality in other fan cultures but the wider reproduction of heterosexuality as ideal. To this end, I will examine the fans' letters more fully as texts in themselves, making them the central focus of analysis.

In the lesbian star/fan relationship we can assert that 'the star makes the fan', because without an idol the fan would not exist. However, we may also say that 'the fan makes the star': without devoted fans who make certain films popular, subscribe to fan magazines and buy the products associated with a film or a star, the star would be 'nothing', the 'star' would not 'be' a star. The construction of identity at a wider level is similar, as it takes place via the relationships between discursive cultural and social practices.

The idea that audiences and texts are simultaneously co-constructed is excellently articulated by Lawrence Grossberg in an article about fandom, in which he argues:

> The relations between culture and audiences cannot be understood simply as the process by which people appropriate already existing texts into the already constituted context of their social position, their experience or their needs. Nor can it be described in terms which suggest that the audience is simply passively acceding to the predetermined nature of the text. In fact, both audiences and texts are continually remade – their identity and effectiveness reconstructed – by relocating their place within different contexts which enable them to consume, interpret and use texts in specific ways.[1]

Thus, in the context of lesbian fandom, both lesbian identities and heterosexual identities are constantly being reproduced in a continually shifting field of social relations, a process which the star/fan system takes part in. For the most part this produces dominant (that is, heterosexual) identities. However, in the lesbian star/fan context, lesbian identities are constructed.

Significantly, white identities are often idealized in this star/fan context. The notion of ethnicity is, thus, also important to me in this chapter. Although I did not inquire about the race or ethnicity of the lesbian fans who wrote to me (and, indeed, none of the correspondents mentioned anything about their own ethnic or racial identities), I believe it is possible to situate their fandom in terms of notions of race and ethnicity. In fact many fans articulated adoration for their idol using racial signifiers: a phenomenon I will examine later in this chapter.

The silence on the issue of race and ethnicity exhibited by my participants is possibly explained by my request for 'lesbian fans', and the fact that I did not ask for any information about their racial or ethnic identity. However, I would also like to suggest that perhaps this silence about ethnic identity indicates that the participants more readily embraced their sexuality than their ethnicity. Furthermore, this may suggest that lesbian fans, and, indeed, fans more widely, consume their idols through the veil of idealism that so often seems to make whiteness disappear into the mists of normativity.

In the different sections of this chapter I will highlight how the construction of heterosexual identities through the conventional notions of sex and gender is challenged by various modes of readership in lesbian fandom. But first it is important to address a number of questions. First, how are classic romantic narratives that are structured by heterosexual conventionality reworked in the structure of a specifically lesbian gaze? Second, how are dominant knowledges about gender and sex disrupted through modes of desire, pleasure and the gaze in lesbian fandom? Third, how are racial or ethnic identities articulated in this context of lesbian romantic narratives structured by a lesbian gaze, and how may such articulations either dislodge or reproduce the whiteness as ideal? Fourth, how can we understand the intersection of the categories of *masculinity* and *woman* as radically disruptive of heterosexuality in this context? Before I examine these ideas in relation to the kinds of lesbian identification and desire articulated in the fan's letters, it is important to understand how the idea of fan culture has been discussed in recent cultural theory.

What is a Fan? What is a Lesbian Fan?

The answer to these questions would seem to be obvious – a fan is someone who adores an idol. Nevertheless, it is crucial to examine how fandom has been discussed in recent cultural theory in order to establish how my analysis of lesbian fandom sits in relation to such theory.

In *Textual Poachers* Henry Jenkins identifies fandom as a signifier of resistance:

Fandom's very existence represents a critique of conventional forms of consumer culture. Yet fandom also provides a space within which fans may articulate their specific concerns about sexuality, gender, racism, colonialism, militarism, and forced conformity. Fandom contains both negative and positive forms of empowerment. Its institutions allow the expression both of what fans are struggling against and what they are struggling for; its cultural products articulate the fans' frustration with their everyday life as well as their fascination with representations that pose alternatives.[2]

In an article entitled 'The Cultural Economy of Fandom' John Fiske argues for the specificity of the fan 'subculture', and in his introductory paragraph provides this informative description of fandom:

Fandom is a common feature of popular culture in industrial societies. It selects from the repertoire of mass-produced and mass-distributed entertainment certain performers, narratives or genres and takes them into the culture of a self-selected fraction of the people. They are then reworked into an intensely pleasurable, intensely signifying popular culture that is both similar to, yet significantly different from, the culture of more 'normal' popular audiences. Fandom is typically associated with cultural forms that the dominant value system denigrates – pop music, romance novels, comics, Hollywood mass-appeal stars (sport, probably because of its appeal to masculinity is an exception). It is thus associated with the cultural tastes of subordinated formations of the people, particularly with those disempowered by any combination of gender, age, class and race.[3]

The fandom of a proportion of lesbian consumers of kd and Martina fits well into both Jenkins's and Fiske's description of what constitutes a fan. Lesbian fans are subordinated through sexuality, and kd is certainly located within what Fiske calls a culturally 'denigrated' form of entertainment – pop music. Martina, on the other hand, is a sporting star. Significantly, sport is not described by Fiske as a culturally denigrated form of entertainment, because in its appeal to masculinity, sport upholds the dominant value system. Fiske actually suggests that *heterosexual* masculinity is what makes sport so popular. Following his analysis, we could say that football appeals to boys and men because of virulent displays of masculinity both on and off the pitch which exalt the conventional heterosexual masculine values of competitiveness, vocality, strength, skill and, often, violence. This appeal of sport to masculinity is useful in understanding the dynamics of Martina's stardom within the tennis circuit. In the context of the lesbian fandom of Martina, sport does contain the possibility for fandom. Moreover, as I have shown, Martina's popularity as a lesbian idol is structured by her masculinity.

The popularity of sport for lesbians, through the adoration of masculinity in lesbian ideals, therefore brings into question Fiske's premise of heterosexuality. He implies that because sport is followed by men, whom he sees as dominant in society (he does not mention black men, or black masculinity), then fandom is not a feature of the sporting domain.[4] The fact that masculinity is what makes sport so popular for lesbians is disruptive at a wider level, disturbing the normative heterosexual imperative traditionally associated with masculinity in sports. For instance, the mass appeal of football stars for boys and men may be read in terms of homosexual desire, in the light of Martina's popularity amongst lesbians.

However, it is also important to remember that lesbians idolize lesbian stars who have been constructed via codes of both masculinity and femininity. For example, as a documentary about *Brookside*'s first lesbian character, Beth Jordache (shown as part of the *Dyke TV* series on Channel 4 in 1995) illustrates, the feminine character of Beth was idolized across the country by lesbian soap opera viewers. Thus, as the gender boundaries of homosexual desires and pleasures are transgressed, and such transgressions are integrated into popular iconography, the idolization of men by men and women by women, in every social arena, begins to signify very differently and forces us to rethink the heterosexualized boundaries of fandom outlined by theorists of fandom.

The Lesbian Fan

At this point it is important to analyse more specifically how lesbian fandom may differ from heterosexual fandom. Fiske, elaborating on the definitive aspects of fandom quoted above, uses the term 'semiotic productivity' to describe how fan cultures produce meanings and pleasures out of the products of the culture industries that relate to their social situation. Thus he suggests that fans create their own subcultures in the form of a 'shadow cultural economy'. Fiske uses Bourdieu's theory of 'cultural capital' (the idea that economic and cultural privilege are radically interconnected) to argue that 'Fandom offers ways of filling cultural lack and provides the social prestige and self-esteem that go with cultural capital.'[5] Thus, Fiske suggests, '"popular" discrimination involves the selection of texts or stars that offer fans opportunities to make meanings of their social identities and social experiences that are self-interested and functional'.[6] Through using Fiske's analysis it is possible to see how lesbian fan practices may lead to cultural empowerment and the sustained reproduction of lesbian identity.

Fiske also maintains that fans are productive in two other ways: first, that some fans engage in 'enunciative productivity' (they produce talk through discussing their idols or favourite soaps); second, he claims that fans also engage in 'textual productivity' by producing further texts (for instance, they may write novels about the extra-textual adventures of idolized characters in television dramas, or write letters to other fans – indeed, the letters I received from lesbian fans would fall into this category).

Of further significance is that lesbian fandom is a development in an expanding lesbian culture. However, because there have been no 'out' lesbian media stars until recently, lesbian fandom as a subculture in itself is a fairly new phenomenon – indeed, it could be described more as a subculture *within a subculture*. Thus it is important to analyse how far lesbian fandom focuses on the issue of lesbian identity itself, in relation to, perhaps different, identificatory emphases which feature in heterosexual fandom.

The following quotes highlight some of the main differences between heterosexual fan culture and lesbian fan culture. The first extract is from a letter sent from one female fan of Barry Manilow to another, and is an example of Fiske's textual productivity:

> Oh God, Mandy, is it so much to ask for to want to bear the child of the man you love with every ounce of your being. I'm going to start work on my poem as the follow up to my fantasy as soon as I've finished work on my labour of love for Barry's Birthday.
>
> > All my love,
> > lashings of Manilust as ever
> > *Julie.*[7]

This, and in fact all the letters about Barry which are reproduced in Fred and Judy Vermorel's article 'A Glimpse of the Fan Factory',[8] are structured by heterosexual desire for Barry Manilow. Some of the themes of these letters are similar to those in my letters from lesbian fans – for example, at live performances Barry fans believed that he was looking straight at them in the audience, and lesbian fans also commented on how they felt they were being personally addressed through kd's songs at live concerts.

So, although there are similarities between heterosexual and lesbian fandom, there are also significant differences between the two. Heterosexual desire structures the letters to Barry, and although lesbian desire structures the letters from lesbian fans, these letters are equally structured by 'coming out' narratives. The following extracts from Sabrina's letter signify that lesbian fandom not only secures lesbian identities it can even make them possible. Sabrina was 14 when she wrote to me, and therefore realized that lesbianism was an option very early in her adult life:

> Everything in my life changed in the summer of '92. I saw an advert for *Ingénue* on the television. It was amazing! This beautiful woman jumped out at me from the screen and two glorious seconds of 'Miss Chatelaine' floated around the room. My exact thoughts were 'God! I'm in love. No! I can't be, it's a woman.' It scared me rigid. I'd never fancied or loved anyone in my life and the fact that kd was a woman nearly killed me from shock.

Sabrina goes on to explain how she subsequently 'came out' as a lesbian:

> Another thing is the expression 'it's just a phase'. Complete *crap*! I suppose I always knew, but I just wouldn't let it out. Funnily enough, I have more confidence in myself and I had enough courage to go out and find myself a girlfriend who I have been with since I was thirteen – that's about ten months ago now. You'd be surprised how many lesbians there are.

Here, Sabrina's swift dismissal of the explanation that her feelings are 'just a phase' shows how her idolization of kd has helped her to counter heterosexual oppression.

As we can see, the media stardom of kd has made her an important role model for teenagers who want to 'come out' as lesbians. Daisy was 27 when she wrote to me, and in this next quote remembers how she began watching her idol, Martina, on television in 1976. Daisy describes how knowing about Martina's lesbianism informed the development of her own lesbian identity in her teenage years:

She had a profound effect on me when I was growing up, especially between the age of thirteen to eighteen. She gave me hope and made me feel good about myself ... being gay was natural for her and it made it acceptable and natural for me too.

Roberta describes how her life changed after she discovered kd lang by chance; indeed, her whole letter concentrates on how her adoration for kd structured her decision to become a lesbian:

I had never heard of her until May 1992 when she sang on *Wogan*. It was quite by chance I happened to be watching ... I glanced up and saw a face that I immediately felt drawn to; it was a strange feeling, like nothing I have ever felt before ... I felt that this moment was the beginning of something very special, something that would change my life ... I had never been physically attracted to a woman (not consciously anyway), and at that time I did not understand my feelings at all. ... Having been married for eight years I thought I must be rather unusual to have these feelings (I know now that I'm not the only one!). It has taken me a while to realize that I am attracted to women – and now realize that I always have been. I feel a different person now, and it's almost as though kd has given me my freedom by making me realize my true self; she has given me so much, and she will always mean a lot to me.

Thus lesbian fandom is structured by the anxieties and frustrations, as well as the rewards and excitement, of becoming and being a lesbian. This 'specialness' that is important to lesbian fans testifies to the strong sense of individuality that being able to come out as a lesbian signifies. Here, feeling 'special' means something very different to a lesbian living in a homophobic culture, and reproducing an identity that is forbidden, than to a straight fan, as I will go on to argue in more detail later.

In this section I have tried to demonstrate that a subculture of lesbian fans does indeed exist within a wider lesbian subculture, and that lesbian fandom empowers lesbians who want to 'come out' as teenagers. It is implausible to imagine that a female Barry Manilow fan, for example, would realize that she was heterosexual because of discovering Barry; heterosexual fandom, rather, reinforces a socially sanctioned heterosexual identity. Heterosexual fandom closes down identity options for fans through securing heterosexuality as an ideal and dominant identity; lesbian fandom, conversely, opens up the range of identities available to the individual. The relative freedom about coming out that Sabrina describes in her letter would not have been available to teenagers ten or twenty years ago, thus the media popularity of kd and Martina has had a powerful influence on how possible it is to be a lesbian in the 1990s, even whilst still at school.

In the next sections I will analyse how the lesbian star/fan relationship is structured by notions of *masculinity* and *romance*. Examining constructions of lesbian masculinity and lesbian romance narratives in the fan letters from my respondents, I will concentrate on how such discursive constructions disturb the idealization of heterosexual identity produced through a sex-to-gender causality that structures heterosexual romantic texts in western culture.

Dangerous Liaisons: Lesbian Romance in the Star/Fan Relationship

In this section I want to discuss the letters sent to me by kd and Martina fans in relation to the discourse of romance. I will argue that in describing their innermost thoughts and feelings about their idols, these fans overturn the heterosexual premise upon which romantic discourse turns. Analysing the letters in the light of a popular understanding of romance within western culture, I will also argue that the lesbian-specific feelings and emotions that are described disrupt the conventional structure of heterosexual love, and that many other key features of the heterosexual romantic text are being rewritten in this lesbian star/fan relationship. In the next section I will go on to argue that romantic discourse is being radically restructured in these lesbian fan letters through the way in which lesbian masculinity is desired through specifically lesbian looking relations.

When I talk about romance in the context of this chapter, I am referring to the long tradition of 'romances': stories of romantic love that embody the idea of 'courtly love', often expressed through chivalric prose narratives, and dating back at least to the Middles Ages. From the 1770s onwards, the literary and philosophical movement of Romanticism drew on a much narrower set of concerns which constructed romantic love in terms of the prevalent social and cultural discourses of the time (Romanticism's link with individualism and the growth of consumerism has been highlighted by Colin Campbell).[9] Its primary mode of expression was poetry. My aim is to set the phenomenon of lesbian romance within this much wider discourse of romantic love.

The lesbian fan letters can be interpreted as romantic texts because they often display a romantic narrative structure. In *Star Gazing* Jackie Stacey has noted that when female fans wrote to her about their female idols, their letters were sometimes structured like romantic narratives. She has also pinpointed the moment when female fans first saw female Hollywood film stars in the 1940s as integral to this narrative structure, and uses a letter from a Deanna Durbin fan as an example:

> Deanna Durbin is introduced here within the discourse of romance. The memory of the first 'meeting', or rather 'sighting', is retold within the structure of a romantic narrative whose sequence of events culminates in the moment of seeing her favourite star on the cinema screen. Its structure is built around a series of gaps, enigmas or absences which is typical of the romance narrative.[10]

Stacey goes on to explain how the fan initially expresses her fascination for the star's face, which was appearing in magazines and newspapers, then hears her voice on the radio, and finally puts a name to the face and the voice. The letter writer goes on to describe how she saw her first Deanna Durbin film when she was 12, as a part of a special treat, and subsequently becomes lost in a description of the extent of her adoration. Stacey claims that 'This step-by-step movement towards the moment of seeing Deanna Durbin offers a structure for the articulation of increasingly intense feelings for the star'.[11] She also argues that this fan's 'memory is not only structured like a romantic narrative but is also characterized by its use of romantic language'.[12]

Stacey's claim is radical indeed. One of her central arguments in *Star Gazing* is that western culture is so saturated with visual images of femininity that the homoerotic desires of female fans for female stars, in a Hollywood star system structured by the idea of femininity as spectacle, seem unavoidable. She argues that although the Deanna Durbin fan declares her heterosexuality, desire between women nevertheless structures this star/fan context:

> The anxiety about the possibility of homoerotic connotations is here expressed through the respondent's heterosexual identity and confirmed by her marital status and reproductive roles. Heterosexuality is thus

invoked to protect against any interpretations, including those which have clearly occurred to this respondent, of such love of another female as containing homoerotic pleasures. The rigid boundary between heterosexuality and homosexuality as two mutually exclusive identities is thus reaffirmed, despite the strength of adoration and love 'for a girl' expressed in this respondent's story. The homoeroticism of such romantic recreations is nevertheless striking in this narrative of 'love at first sight'.[13]

The letters about the lesbian stars kd and Martina display a similar structure to the letter by the Deanna Durbin fan. There is an equally important focus on the unravelling of the letter as a 'love story', the star as a spectacle for visual pleasures and the use of romantic language, as a lengthy extract from this lesbian fan letter illustrates:

Everything in my life changed in the summer of 1992. I saw an advert for *Ingénue* on the television. It was amazing! This beautiful woman jumped out at me from the screen and two glorious seconds worth of 'Miss Chatelaine' floated around the room. My exact thoughts were 'God! I'm in love. No! I can't be, it's a woman!' It scared me rigid. I'd never fancied or loved anyone in my life and the fact that kd was a woman nearly killed me from shock. Actually when I was seven I saw a woman working in a jewellery store and I didn't know whether I fancied her or just thought she was pretty.

I spent a month glued to the television waiting for that advert to appear again, and I was delighted when it did. Although by this stage I was helplessly lost, I refused to buy *Ingénue* because I was scared about the fact I might be a lesbian.

Two months later I was on holiday and I was at a market. Two men were running a stall with loads of pirated tapes for £2.50 each. There was *Ingénue*, insistently sitting at the back of the table. I didn't realise I had bought it until I got half way down the road.

A week later I plucked up the courage to play it. It sounds stupid that a tape could frighten someone, but I was terrified. I listened to it carefully. Once, twice, three times ... five, yes, five hours later I turned it off. I didn't love kd but I loved her voice and her music. Wrong! After a week I was lost. I went mad when kd lang was doing the AIDS day concert and it was televised, when she was on BBC 1 (or 2, I can't remember) on *Unplugged* and also when she did a song with Tony

Bennett for his *Unplugged*. Those are the only video recordings. I also own *A Truly Western Experience* (which I had to have imported because it wasn't on sale in the UK anymore), *Shadowland*, *Absolute Torch and Twang* and obviously *Ingénue*. I have a book on kd called *All You Get Is Me* and I've read it twice. Anything that catches my eye with kd on I buy, photocopy or listen to.

People tell me I *thought* I fell in love with kd lang because I'd never fallen for anyone and that caused me to think about my sexuality. As kd is a lesbian they thought I just immediately related to her and tricked myself into falling in love. That's wrong. I had been totally in love with her a year before I even found out that she is gay.

(Sabrina)

In this extract the indicators of a romance narrative pointed out by Stacey are certainly present. There is a step-by-step account of how the fan 'fell in love' with kd, and the use of romantic language highlights the intensity of her feelings: phrases such as 'by this stage I was helplessly lost' underscore Sabrina's heightened emotional state. Gaps, absences and enigmas, which Stacey argues are characteristic of romantic narratives, are also apparent in this letter. Sabrina reports how she didn't notice herself actually buying *Ingénue*, and only realized when she had left the market stall, a typical example of how 'lost moments' structure romantic texts.

Sabrina's idolization of kd is also set up as an enigma: the inexplicability of how she fell in love with a star whom she didn't know was a lesbian, and then became a lesbian herself, is structured by those lost moments and step-by-step memories described by Stacey as typical of the romance narrative. However, Sabrina's letter differs strikingly from the letters Stacey has analysed, as she talks openly about how she became a lesbian because she discovered kd, and how her love for the star was dependent upon her new feelings of lesbian desire and identification. Whereas Stacey suggests that an *implicit* homoeroticism structures the letters from female fans of the 1940s and 1950s female Hollywood stars, an *explicit* lesbian identity characterizes the letters of lesbian fans. Thus, conventional heterosexual romantic discourse is being rewritten, and disrupted, in a specifically lesbian context.

In *Romance Revisited*, Lynne Pearce and Jackie Stacey argue that feminists have engaged with romance in terms of its 'fictionality',[14] and as a discourse that is open to being rewritten in ways which may radically undermine a traditional, white heterosexual romantic narrative structure:[15]

> So, how *does* romantic love, an emotional configuration that most of us experience in a hot confusion of sickness and delight, continue to do so well? The answer ... is that romance survives because of its *narrativity*. In the same way that romantic love may be thought of as a phenomenon which (as Sue Vice observes in her chapter) is 'always already written', so it is liable to perpetual *re-writing*; and it is its capacity for 're-scripting' that has enabled it to flourish at the same time that it has been transformed.[16]

They go on to cite the main components of the classic romantic narrative and suggest that the romantic story offers 'the potential of a heterosexual love union whose fulfilment is threatened by a series of barriers or problems',[17] a characteristic that was evident in Sabrina's fan letter. Pearce and Stacey also claim that the romantic story is a 'quest' for love, where the pleasure for the audience or reader lies in the solution. Often there is a separation, threat of death or actual death which intensifies both textual desire and audience involvement. Further, they add, there is also the possibility of transformation: 'The possibility of becoming "someone else" through a romantic relationship is most certainly one of the most interesting and positive ingredients in its appeal.'[18]

In romantic fiction the first meeting, or the first sight of the object of desire, is also always deeply significant. In Charlotte Brontë's classic romantic novel *Jane Eyre*, which was first published in 1847, and is very much part of the Romantic literary tradition,[19] there is a first meeting of great significance. As Jane walks across a moonlit hilltop, she believes she has seen a mythical animal spirit figure, a Gytrash; however, it turns out to be her future hero Mr Rochester, who falls with his horse to the ground. Jane describes her first sight of him thus:

> Something of daylight still lingered, and the moon was waxing bright; I could see him plainly. His figure was enveloped in a riding cloak, fur collared and steel clasped; its details were not apparent, but I traced the general points of middle height, and considerable breadth of chest. He had a dark face, with stern features and a heavy brow; his eyes and gathered eyebrows looked ireful and thwarted just now; he was

past youth, but had not reached middle age; perhaps he might be thirty-five. I felt no fear of him, and but little shyness.[20]

The detail employed here regarding his 'middle height', 'breadth of chest', 'dark face', 'stern features', 'heavy brow' and 'gathered eyebrows' emphasizes the impact that this first look has on her, and also sets up the romance for the reader.

In contemporary mass-market romantic novels, the first sight of the hero also marks a highly significant moment in the narrative, and is often accompanied by excessive romantic language, as these two quotes from random[21] Mills and Boon novels illustrate:

> As she drew closer her attention was caught by a tall, dark-suited man standing slightly apart from the rest, and her eyes lingered with brief curiosity. Broad-chiselled facial bone-structure in profile provided an excellent foil for the patrician slope of his nose and rugged sculptured jaw.
>
> In his mid-thirties, she judged, aware there was something about his stance that portrayed an animalistic sense of power – a physical magnetism that was riveting.[22]

> He really was a very handsome specimen, she thought admiringly as he stepped out of the water to dry off in the sun. He was tall and lithe, and from the look of him he either cut down trees or built roads for a living, for his muscles had been rippling powerfully. Or else he was just a secret weight-lifter. Whatever he was, a fusty scholar like Zachariah Bennett would probably recoil in horror at such virility: the man's shoulders wide and strong, golden hair glinting on his bronzed chest, his stomach taut and flat, and his hips and thighs ... Apollo himself couldn't have looked better![23]

In both these passages a conventional heterosexual theme is textually secured within the discourse of romance and the representation of the hero via excessive signifiers of masculinity.

As I have illustrated in relation to Sabrina's letter, *traces* of the romantic narrative also characterize the lesbian star/fan relationship. But, despite this, a specifically lesbian exchange is being constructed that challenges the conventional heterosexual discourse of romantic love – the unfolding romantic narrative in Sabrina's letter is as much about her becoming a lesbian as it is about her adoration for kd. Thus, the idea of becoming someone else, highlighted by Pearce and Stacey as a component of traditional romantic narratives, is rewritten in this lesbian context as a desire to become a lesbian.

The Only One

In the lesbian romantic exchange the interconnection of same and other through the interconnection of desire and identification undercuts the regulative function of the heterosexual romantic narrative – namely, to secure women as passive and men as active in a matrix of hierarchical difference premised on the same/other dualism, where desire and identification are kept separate.

Another way that the lesbian fan letters disrupt heterosexual romantic texts is, as I suggested earlier, in the fans' belief that they are individual or 'special', as this quote from kd fan Zoe illustrates: 'I wasn't aware of anyone else having such die-hard, or red hot desires towards her.' The following extract from June's letter also recounts a feeling of 'specialness':

> It was while she sang 'Outside Myself' ... that I just felt completely ... I don't know how to describe it, I wasn't aware of anything else in the room at all, she just seemed to put so much into that song; just thinking about it now makes me feel the same way and every time I hear it (especially the live version) ... I really can't think how to describe how it makes me feel, it just makes my stomach go into a knot. It's very hard to explain without sounding stupid. Anyway, it was after that song I realised I was now one of those strange lesbians who were totally obsessed with kd lang.

Thus in the context of lesbian fandom feeling special may be as much to do with being, or becoming, a lesbian as it is about being a part of a romantic exchange – indeed, one of the most prominent feelings about discovering you are a lesbian must be the realization that you are quite different from most, if not all, of those around you. Hence, the 'specialness' that marks lesbianism apart from heterosexuality counteracts the dominant heterosexual understanding of romance, and heterosexual forms of idolization.

This rearticulation of romantic specialness, via the specificity of a lesbian romantic narrative, undermines the regulatory drive of heterosexual romantic narratives, because it is lesbianism – a socially unsanctioned identity – that is being idolized and reproduced here, appropriating a romantic notion of specialness that normally operates in a heterosexual context to underline the deviance of lesbianism. Further, this resistant specialness of lesbian desire displaces the importance of the active-same/passive-other binary in the heterosexual romantic narrative, because it is lesbian *masculinity* that is desired and adored. Thus, the object of lesbian desire in this context is highly androgynous, and subsequently cannot be othered in terms of a heterosexual knowledge system.

The Look of Love

The first sight of their idols is described in the letters in great detail, and occupies an important place in the narrative structure as a whole, as it sets up the space for a more in-depth discussion of the fan's feelings for the idol. The importance of the first sight exemplifies how traces of romantic discourse pervade the lesbian narratives in these letters.

> The first time I ever saw or heard of kd lang was when she was on the *Red Hot and Blue* programme.
> (June)

> It was only really two years ago I got into kd lang, I remember the first time I saw her it was on *Wogan*.
> (Kim)

The process of repeated viewing was also important in the descriptions of the lesbian fan's desire for their idols:

> I noticed her eyes, gorgeous, and kind of cat-like expression. She excites and amazes me with her voice and her looks. When I saw *Salmonberries*, I was struck again by her physical beauty.
> (Freda)

> Every time I saw her on court I admired her more and more – her grace, speed, athleticism, talent – she played awesome tennis – and I considered her more attractive each time.
> (Lisa)

The memory of first hearing kd sing in the fans' narratives also structures their romantic desire for her. The following quote shows how the adoration of kd's voice is central to the romantic narrative structure of Roberta's fan letter:

> I glanced up and saw a face that I immediately felt drawn to, it was a strange feeling, like nothing I have felt before – was it a boy or a woman? And then she sang, I've never heard such a beautiful voice … she didn't just sing, she performed.

Here, then, the importance of the first sighting (or hearing) of the lesbian idol has a specifically lesbian meaning. The fans' excitement can be explained by the fact that there are so few lesbians represented in the media. There may be a perpetual trickle of lesbian characters in soap operas, or in magazines, but to see a 'real' lesbian on the television is incredibly important for lesbian audiences, as it reproduces, and sanctions, their own hard-won, lived-out lesbian identity and culture.

The alternative securing of lesbianism through a heterosexual narrative works with but also on and against the very premise of heterosexual romantic narratives. The relationship of an active male protagonist who looks at a passive female recipient of his desire is dislodged from the centre of the romantic narrative by the dynamics of a lesbian gaze which is structured by the vision of the masculine woman, the notion of androgyny and the spectre of gender misrecognition.

The Language of Love

Another characteristic of the conventional romantic text, as I suggested above, is the use of excessively romantic language. The use of such language is also characteristic of the lesbian fan letter, but in a way that illuminates the disruptive process of the lesbian romantic narrative. Kim writes about Martina:

> in our household we were speechless, almost in tears as Conchita Martinez won match point. What finally got to me was when she reached down and took a piece of turf from centre court knowing it would be her last time in the competition. I felt privileged to watch her last match, a great loss to the world of tennis ... last week a programme was on BBC 1 called *Martina, Farewell to a Champion* I taped it to keep always. I felt a deep anger towards Judy Nelson, Martina's ex-partner ...

Kim's choice of words – 'speechless', 'a great loss' and 'a deep anger' – emphasizes intense desire and adoration. However, the use of this kind of excessive language also represents the emotional intensity that structures the experience of living as a lesbian in a homophobic society, and expresses both the excitement of finally finding a lesbian star to idolize and the threat that trauma poses in the personal lives of such devotedly followed lesbian stars – witness the anger Kim felt towards Judy Nelson. In another letter, June described an audio tape of kd in a way that recalls Kim's description: 'My most treasured possession is the tape off the radio of the live concert I was at – I've made a backup copy just in case it ever gets damaged – I really would be heartbroken. It just brings back so many memories.' June also mentioned the intense feeling of pleasure she experienced at one of kd's live concerts: 'every time she smiled I just crumpled into my chair like a pathetic rag or something'.

June's description of herself as a 'pathetic rag' acknowledges how kd can reduce her lesbian fans to 'useless wrecks' because she is a *masculine woman*. Thus the intensity of the response of women to masculinity, characteristic of heterosexual romantic narratives, is alternatively reproduced here to evoke desire between women in a specifically lesbian context. Here, the symbol of the heterosexual masculine figure of conventional romance stories is disrupted by the fact that, in a lesbian context, the masculine figure does not impose a placing of the desiring woman (lesbian) in a position of passive femininity as the recipient of the heterosexualizing active male gaze. Instead, in a lesbian context, these heterosexual visual signifiers of romantic othering are displaced by the interconnection of desire and identification in the romantic moment. This is not to suggest, however, that the lesbian star and the lesbian fan are interlocked in a narcissistic bind; on the contrary, difference between them is structured through that very star/fan relationship. The idea that difference can only be achieved via a heterosexualized sex-gender binary framework, or else desire is narcissistic, is heterosexually reductive in the extreme.

A Fantastic Journey

Fantasies and dreams are also prominent in the letters. Such fantasies are also, often, particularly romantic. Roberta describes how she daydreams about kd lang, and then relates a specific fantasy scenario:

> kd's face and voice were in my mind all the time – I would even wake up in the night with her singing in my head. I would daydream about her for hours. ... If I met kd I would want to tell her how special she is to me, and why – but I would probably be speechless with nerves – or maybe I would just jump on her and give her a big snog!! (Only joking ... I think!)

Roberta speculates about some of the things she might do if she ever met her idol, but fantasy scenarios can be much more detailed, often focusing on some sort of romantic encounter: 'The main thing I wander off daydreaming about is getting to know her – and of course I always imagine she's a very nice person and we'd get along like a house on fire so eventually we'd end up leaping into bed.' (June)

Some of the fantasy scenarios are extremely creative and original. Vicky even made a reference to a brand of coffee that she had seen advertised on television. The adverts for Gold Blend® coffee show different stages of a budding heterosexual romance; in her letter Vicky subverts the heterosexual romantic theme of these adverts by substituting a romance between herself and her idol:

> If I ever saw kd lang I think I'd pass out first and when I've recovered from fainting (hopefully kd would come to my aid) I would ask her to my place for a cup of Gold Blend® coffee. During coffee I would most definitely chat her up and try to get her phone number. I wouldn't try and get her into bed because I really respect her.

Ironically, since Vicky wrote this letter, these coffee adverts have received a satirical treatment on Channel 4's *Dyke TV* (summer of 1996); renaming the beverage 'Dyke Blend' the programme followed a budding lesbian romance over a series of several adverts.

Other fantasy scenarios involved the wish to go back and experience something that actually happened in the idol's early career: 'Sometimes I wish I could go back in time, be a little older and watch her play a final against Chris Evert – that would be a dream.' (Daisy, a Martina fan)

Kim's night-time dreaming about kd lang extended into a daytime fantasy:

> I dreamed once about singing on stage a cover version of 'Constant Craving' and who came up on stage to join in but kd herself, we became great friends (ah ... dreams), if I did ever meet her I'd say 'I'll play if you sing', I guess it's my ambition to be on stage with kd lang, who knows?

In some letters I received, however, fantasy scenarios involved much more than merely describing what a fan would say or do if they met their idol. For some lesbian fans, such as Lisa, fantasy had obviously played an integral part in their lives, and proved to be a constant source of pleasure. Fantasy heavily structured Lisa's desires for idols throughout her life. She wrote to me about Martina, but began by talking about how fantasy had structured her life since the age of nine:

> When I was nine or so I had 'daydreams' – knight in armour rescues maiden, gunfighter defeats bad guy, wins girl, that kind of thing – and it was always someone famous I rode off into the sunset with (that was as far as it got then – at nine I didn't know what came after the swooning kiss and the ride off!). It would be whichever actress had captured my fancy for that particular week – Sophia Loren, Brigitte Bardot, Cyd Hayman – very discriminating tastes I had in those days. Then in my late teens – by now an 'out' (officially) dyke and knowing where to take the fantasies – along came Suzi Quatro.

Lisa's long history of producing fantasy scenarios enabled her to successfully construct elaborate fantasies about Martina:

> By the mid-1980s she was one of my main 'fantasy life' targets. Not that I still did the knight-in-armour routine. No, more like bumping into her at tennis matches and knocking the rackets out of her hand, picking them up and going on from there. Always cool, calm, irresistible. ... Walks on beaches, candlelit dinners, log fires, etc. etc. I always knew what to do, what to say. I also was always the perfect lover, wonderful in bed (as was she) and of course she fell hopelessly in love with me ...

Here, fantasizing about Martina, Lisa becomes the 'perfect lover', a transformation which recalls the narrative of romantic stories, when the heroine finally sees herself through the hero's eyes as the perfect woman she always wanted to be.

However, many fans emphasized that they had 'real' lives and lovers outside their fantasy lives. In many instances they would refer to their real-life lovers after relating a fantasy scenario. Occasionally, a conflict of interest emerged for the fan between the fantasy experience with their idol and their real-life partner. Sometimes the fan would be quite clear that the 'real' lover was preferred; sometimes it would be the idol. Lisa, having described her fantasy life in great detail, swiftly added:

> If this portrays me as a bleary-eyed fantasist doing nothing all day except dream of making love with Martina – well that's not too accurate. I don't only daydream of Martina, and I don't daydream all

the time. I work (shift-work) I go to evening classes (when I can) I dance – I go to a country music club and do line dancing. I go to discos. I date, I fall in love, break up, listen to music, read ...

Lisa also referred to her real-life love, though still talking of Martina, in this quote I used to introduce the chapter:

if by some miracle she did find me, and just cocked her little finger at me and said 'come' – I'd go. Wherever she led. Whatever it cost. Abandon job, house, the lot. Because there's just no one else like her, anywhere (except of course, if the woman I'm in love with beckoned in the other direction!)

In the extracts from Lisa's letter we can see how, in a fantasy experience, the person creating the fantasy can feel in control of a situation that in real life they may find daunting. Through fantasy experiences, fans can feel positive about themselves, and, moreover, important to their idol. Identification works in the fantasy scenario through the production of a specifically *lesbian* fantasy, and a specifically *lesbian* desire is constructed through fantasy. Moreover, through this generative space of lesbian fantasy both lesbian identifications and lesbian identity are strengthened and reproduced.

Lesbian fantasy romances are characterized by an interconnection of lesbian identification (the lesbian identity of the fan is being strengthened) and desire for the lesbian idol (by strengthening lesbian identification in this context, lesbian desire may be expressed). Thus, these are also spaces through which modes of lesbian desire do not require an articulation of the woman as passive other. In these fantasies conventional notions of masculinity and femininity combine in order to express lesbian desire: for example, Lisa's fantasies contain stories about seducing her idols and being seduced by them. The fact that the idol is a masculine woman undercuts the structure of gendered othering that traditionally sanctions heterosexuality in romantic narrative.

The Lesbian and the Obstacle

Another feature of romantic texts is 'the obstacle', or obstacles, which stand in the way of the development of the romance. In romantic novels obstacles hinder the relationship between the hero and heroine and also structure the reader's pleasures – for example, a hero may be unattainable to the heroine because she is 'unattractive' or not his social equal. This notion of unattainability also structures fandom generally: the idol is unattainable to the fan.

Despite this, some fans of kd or Martina nevertheless believe that they will meet their idol and a romance will develop. Some believe that their idol will notice their qualities of goodness and loyalty, and choose them over the more famous women they may come into contact with during their careers (such as Cindy Crawford, perhaps). This self-defined integrity of the lesbian fan relates to the same idea of selfhood favoured by the heroine of the romantic novel. But this integrity is quite specific to lesbian culture, and relates to living according to a distinct, if variable, value system as a lesbian. Thus, loyalty and respect felt by the fan for the star is also a respect for the way that star lives as a lesbian in a homophobic society. The following extracts about kd illustrate the lesbian fan's quest for a romance with their idols:

> My thoughts about my future grew more towards the desire to meet her; I truly longed to kiss this woman.
>
> (Zoe)

> I dream that her life will only be complete when she meets me and we become lovers. I feel love, desire, passion for her as well as unlimited respect and admiration. She has the allure of being unobtainable while seeming like someone you could really know.
>
> (Annie)

As I have illustrated, lesbian fan letters are, in a sense, romantic narratives, yet they are also, importantly, lesbian texts – full of stories of self-discovery, lesbian recognition, lesbian desire and lesbian identifications. They are part of lesbian culture, and as such disrupt the heterosexual romantic narrative within which the woman is the passive other, the recipient of a regulating romantic male gaze. In the lesbian star/fan relationship lesbian identification and desire interlink to produce a site of transformation where gender ambiguity, gender misrecognition and the vision of the masculine woman combine to make the romantic scenario *both* a place of alternative significance (a specifically lesbian romantic narrative) *and* a space where the regulation imposed by heterosexual notions of sex and gender difference is displaced. The way that traces of romance resonate within these lesbian texts, disrupting a heterosexual imperative which we associate with romantic media genres, must make us reconsider how we think about romance and evaluate the disparate fields of cultural practice where romantic conventions may be challenged and rewritten.

'The Butch Side of the Line': The Spectacle of Masculinity and the Lesbian Gaze

> You asked how Martina had influenced me. I stopped being worried about being on the butch side of the line (not that I really like stereotypes but no one will ever call me feminine!) and I stopped caring about what other people thought if I worked out in the gym! She does it, so can I!
>
> *(Lisa)*

In Chapter Three I argued that Martina's body may be read through conventional codes of masculinity, and that the figure of the masculine woman she epitomizes disrupts the heterosexual equation of masculinity with men. Central to this argument was the idea that she is desired by her fans for this masculine 'look'. In this section I want to illustrate how the lesbian gaze undercuts heterosexual looking relations that are premised on regulatory notions of sex and gender difference.

The quote from Lisa, above, illustrates how Martina's fans identify with her through the notion of a specific form of masculinity within lesbian culture – butchness. In the previous section of this chapter I argued that lesbian fan letters trouble a dominant heterosexual romantic narrative structure, whilst also drawing on some of its key features. In this section I want to suggest that these romantic traces are deeply underscored by a pervasive visual indicator of lesbian desire, identification, recognition and culture – the vision of the masculine woman.

In letters about Martina much emphasis is placed on her body, particularly on her muscular physique; however, in letters about kd, dress, style and facial structure are more important. These different emphases may be read as a desire amongst the lesbian fans for different constructions of masculinity, in relation both to their idols and themselves. This extract from Kim's letter illustrates how kd is desired because of a form of masculinity that is signified by the wearing of suits: 'last year I watched a concert in aid of the "Terrence Higgins Trust", the clothes she wore I felt didn't suit her, in fact they made her look frumpy, not the gorgeous way she looks in a suit'.

In this section I will frame a discussion of lesbian masculinity within the discourses of 'looking' and 'spectacle' that have structured both the analysis of the Hollywood star system in the twentieth century and of western consumer culture more generally.

The Art of Looking

Since the publication in 1975 of Laura Mulvey's influential article 'Visual Pleasure and Narrative Cinema'[24] feminist film theorists have become familiar with her general premise: that looking relations in Hollywood cinema are constructed through a patriarchal system of sexual difference, whereby the woman on screen is the object of, and spectacle for, the 'male gaze' of both the male on-screen protagonist and the male off-screen spectator. To illustrate her theory Mulvey uses a psychoanalytic framework.

In 1981 Mulvey herself offered a reworking of her original position in 'Afterthoughts on "Visual Pleasure and Narrative Cinema" ...'.[25] In this follow-up article, Mulvey examines possibilities for female spectatorship. Nevertheless, she merely articulates female spectatorship through the process of heterosexualized masculinization. She argues that the female is only offered the position of spectator when she views the film *as if she were a man*. Mulvey's dependence on a framework of psychoanalysis is clearly in evidence here – in psychoanalytic theory, all pleasures revolve around the axis of male desire.

Many feminist film theorists (and feminist theorists concerned with the issue of representation more generally) who come from the cultural studies tradition rather than the psychoanalytic camp have argued that specifically feminine spectatorship pleasures that do not rely on hetero-sexualized masculinization or narcissistic identification, do exist. An edited collection entitled *The Female Gaze* examines the problem that was set up by Mulvey. In the book's introduction the editors have this to say about Mulvey's notion of the 'male gaze':

> Mulvey's thesis states that visual pleasure in mainstream Hollywood cinema derives from and reproduces a structure of male looking/female to-be-looked-at-ness (whereby the spectator is invited to identify with a male gaze at an objectified female). This pleasure, she concludes, must be disrupted in order to facilitate a feminist cinema. Mulvey's article paved the way for a great deal of interesting work on the

representation of woman. Unfortunately, however, the notion of a 'male gaze' as dominant in all mainstream genres has since become something of an orthodoxy.[26]

In an article in this volume about female spectatorship pleasures, 'Desperately Seeking Difference', Jackie Stacey examines the films *Desperately Seeking Susan*[27] and *All About Eve*[28] in order to challenge the validity of psychoanalytic frameworks for analysing looking relations between women in the cinema:

> Both *Desperately Seeking Susan* and *All About Eve* tempt the woman spectator with the fictional fulfilment of becoming an ideal feminine other, while denying complete transformation by insisting upon differences between women. The rigid distinction between either desire or identification, so characteristic of psychoanalytic film theory, fails to address the construction of desires which involve a specific interplay of both processes.[29]

Here, Stacey opens up possibilities for analysing homoerotic pleasures and desires between women in on-screen narratives, and in female spectatorship.

In her later book, *Star Gazing*, Stacey develops her analysis of female looking pleasures in relation to the cinema. Here, she examines the pleasures taken by British female fans of 1940s and 1950s female film stars, pinpointing the difference between a textual approach, where the spectator is determined by the film text itself, and an approach which recognizes the pleasures, desires and identifications of members of the cinema audience:

> The reluctance to engage with questions of cinema audiences, for fear of dirtying one's hands with empirical material, has led to an inability to think about active female desire beyond the limits of masculine positionings. By introducing the female spectator (in the cinema) into the equation, I would argue that there are cultural meanings associated with women looking at glamorous feminine ideals that differ from those ascribed to men. Given the saturation of this culture with images of attractive femininity, what might be the specificity of women's relationship to such desirable images beyond the psychoanalytic options of masculinisation or narcissism?[30]

I use 'empirical material' (fans accounts) in my analysis to demonstrate how lesbian fans consume lesbian stars in a diverse array of media contexts. Such an approach has been enabled by the continuing work of feminist film theorists, such as Stacey, who concentrate on practices of looking between women. Studies of 'the gaze' in feminist film theory are important to my study, as I want to argue that there is a *lesbian gaze* in the lesbian star/fan context. In order to analyse this phenomenon, it is critical to acknowledge the different kinds of looking relations that exist in the media texts where kd and Martina are represented and consumed. I also want to explore the issue of the 'live' performances of kd and Martina and how looking relations in such contexts differ from those in the cinema.

The Lesbian Gaze[31]

The most significant difference between looking relations in the cinema context and looking relations in representations of kd is that the 'on-screen' gaze is often cut out of the picture: kd does not usually sing *to* someone else (as a hero would speak to a heroine in a Hollywood film). kd sings directly to an audience at her live performances and when she appears on music or chat shows. If she appears in a documentary programme, an interviewer, who is often represented as just a voice, stands in for the audience. The relationship to the interviewer does not amount to a narrative in itself; its purpose is information gathering (although documentaries often have a narrative structure, opening, perhaps, with the beginning of a star's career). kd's speech, and gaze, in such programmes is vicariously directed at the home viewer, and the home viewer's gaze is directed at kd in return. A similar format was used in a recent documentary about Martina entitled *Martina: Farewell To A Champion*, screened in Britain on BBC 1 in 1995. Although the dynamics of the gaze in these contexts may differ from the cinematic context, they do facilitate possibilities for feelings of specialness and other constructions of desire in the lesbian fans.

In kd's video collection *Harvest of Seven Years*, she occasionally sings to 'us', but sometimes addresses someone within the narrative of the video. An example of this is the song 'So in Love'. Directed by Percy Adlon (who also directed her in *Salmonberries*), this song tells the story of a lesbian couple. In this case the looking relations are quite similar to those employed in narrative cinema. In *Salmonberries* the on-screen lesbian gaze between kd (Kotzebue) and Rosel Zech (Roswitha) is constructed within a romantic narrative. Thus this film is important both in terms of the construction of romance between the characters and between kd and the lesbian audience through a specific lesbian gaze.

The textual form through which Martina has most often been represented is the television coverage of her tennis matches. Before her retirement Martina would be on British television screens every year at Wimbledon. This context of regular television tennis coverage is important in terms of looking relations. kd's performances fit comfortably into the way singing stars are traditionally represented in show business, and, thus, distinctions and similarities between these media contexts and the cinema context are relatively easy to ascertain. We could also say that Martina acts in a kind of narrative in her tennis matches. Significantly, this is not a narrative in which one character is depicted as desiring feminine ideals, which Stacey argues goes on in *Desperately Seeking Susan*,[32] or a narrative within which a lesbian romance develops, such as *Salmonberries*. It might be more appropriate to compare the tennis match narrative with the masculine cinematic narrative of the shoot-out in a spaghetti western.[33]

Spaghetti westerns are quite a particular film genre. From a European tradition of avant-garde cinema, they strictly adhere to a classic western revenge narrative, and are quite distinct from Hollywood westerns. For example, they contain long periods without speech, in which the tension is dramatically built up. The narratives of the tennis match and spaghetti westerns are similar in several ways. First, Martina's matches have often involved some kind of revenge theme, most notably in her sustained on-court rivalry with Chris Evert in the early 1980s (off-court, the two enjoyed perfectly amicable relations). Spaghetti westerns traditionally establish the narrative via the hero's flashbacks. Similarly, the beginning of tennis coverage usually contains a series of flashbacks to previous matches or tournaments. Thus, in both contexts the battle is set up through a similar use of temporality.

Individual tennis matches also have a strong narrative structure of their own. The narrative closure signified by the final of every Wimbledon tournament is similar to the shoot-out scene which usually characterizes the narrative closure of spaghetti westerns.[34] In both cases the competitors enter the fight scene. In each case they warm up by looking across at their opponent(s). In the western there is a short time before the shoot-out takes place when an audience knows they are not ready to fight. This is equivalent to the warm-up in tennis. After this initial 'looking phase' something changes: in the western, the cinematic scene is closed down through many close-up shots of cowboys eyes, mouths and so on; in tennis, close-ups of the players also have an important function in the coverage of the play. Then the fight is on and, in both cases, there is always only one winner.

In the media contexts within which kd and Martina are represented we can read their images through the cinematic theory of the gaze; this is true of the film *Salmonberries*, but there are also implicit similarities between the cinematic context and the tennis match, the live performance, the documentary, as well as the photographic images I analysed in the previous two chapters. Thus, in the particular context of lesbian stardom and fandom, an array of media contexts act as spaces of consumption where pleasures, desires and romantic narratives are produced through the notion of a lesbian gaze. The gaze that is most important to my analysis in this chapter is the way that lesbian fans look at their lesbian idols.

These next two quotes from Martina fans exemplify the lesbian gaze and the specific interrelationship between this contextualized gaze and conventional ideas about masculinity. In the first quote we can see how the lesbian gaze is structured by the concept of butchness. In the second quote, however, the lesbian gaze is structured by a derisory account of femininity in relation to Martina's more masculine image:

The reasons why I think Martina is beautiful are hard to explain. I think she is really, really sexy. I think it must be because she's so butch ... I'd always watch her and study every part of her body really carefully when she was on TV. I'd watch her shoulders covered by that sexy T-shirt, and look at where her thighs met the line of her underwear. ... She doesn't even have to speak, we don't need words, we just need to *see* her!

(Sadie)

I wasn't so keen on the long hair she had for a while. I didn't think it suited her. Especially when she went 'over the top' in some interviews and some advertising spreads she did – soft fluffy blouses, too much make-up. I didn't find her so attractive then. I would think 'she can try and be as femme as she likes but it won't work – certain sections of the community will revile her for what she is, she might as well just be herself'. I liked her best just as she came on to court, or while she was playing and enjoying herself, not getting tense. ... Or in the interviews where she'd showered and changed but she was between matches so still in sports wear.

(Lisa)

In this next quote, June also describes her idol kd through a derisory account of the conventional codes of femininity, codes which she associates more with Annie Lennox: 'Pictures of kd show her wearing jeans and 'normal' sorts of clothes, whereas Annie always seems to wear weirdy arty type clothes that I can't relate to, and make-up – Annie always plastered herself in make-up and kd doesn't.'

This next quote from Miranda's letter about Martina exemplifies how the desire for lesbian masculinity in a lesbian lover may also structure the lesbian gaze:

I liked all of her body, but especially her hands. As a piano player I always notice people's hands, and can fall in love with someone for their hands, even if it's the only part of their body I find attractive. Her hands are muscular and veined, my favourite type of hands. They look so strong and capable, she seems like someone I could depend on because of her hands, if we were lovers. Now as an out lesbian I think hands are very important for lesbians as we make love with our hands. Our hands are like a sex organ. Heterosexuals have sex with penises and vaginas which are always hidden, but someone's hands are always public. If I met a woman with strong hands I'd think she must be a good lover. I'm sure Martina is very good in bed. I imagine her to be very butch, in command, but also gentle. I don't think she would be a 'do-me queen' who would just lie back and wait.

This fan's idolization of Martina's masculinity, of her 'muscular and veined' hands, draws on specific knowledges about the importance of hands in lesbian sexual practice and also disrupts the dominant discourse, in which gender and sex differences are reproduced in order to constitute heterosexual desire. In idolizing Martina's hands, in the lesbian star/fan context, women are desiring masculinity, but a masculinity that is inscribed upon a female body.

Although Martina's fans idolize her for her masculinity, they were never in doubt about her female identity. In the case of kd however, many fans recalled how they had initially thought she was a man: 'I glanced up and saw a face that I immediately felt drawn to, it was a strange feeling, like nothing I have felt before – was it a boy or a woman? And then she sang, I've never heard such a beautiful voice ...' (Roberta, a kd fan)

Confusion about the gender of an object of desire is quite a well-documented phenomenon within lesbian literature. Virginia Woolf's novel *Orlando*,[35] is an example of how desire may be articulated through gender ambiguity. This fictional 'biography' begins with the protagonist, Orlando, as a young man in Elizabethan England, and progresses to the twentieth century. One day Orlando wakes up to find that he has become a woman. The differences Orlando experiences as a man and as a woman structure the narrative. The following extract describes the first meeting between the male Orlando and Sasha, the Russian princess, and illustrates the erotic nature of gender ambiguity:

> he beheld, coming from the pavilion of the Muscovite Embassy, a figure, which, whether boy's or woman's, for the loose tunic and trousers of the Russian fashion served to disguise the sex, filled him with the highest curiosity. The person, whatever the name or sex, was about middle height, very slenderly fashioned, and dressed entirely in oyster-coloured velvet, trimmed with some unfamiliar greenish-coloured fur. But these details were obscured by the extraordinary seductiveness which issued from the whole person. Images, metaphors of the most extreme and extravagant twined and twisted in his mind. He called her a melon, a pineapple, an olive tree, an emerald, and a fox in the snow all in the space of three seconds; he did not know whether he had heard her, tasted her, seen her, or all three together. ... When the boy, for alas, a boy it must be – no woman could skate with such speed and vigour – swept almost on tiptoe past him, Orlando was ready to tear his hair with vexation that the person was of his own sex, and thus all embraces were out of the question. But the skater came closer. Legs, hands, carriage, were a boy's, but no boy ever had a mouth like that; no boy had those breasts; no boy had eyes which looked as if they had been fished from the bottom of the sea.[36]

The intensity of Orlando's feelings for Sasha at this poignant 'first sight' encounter are illustrated in his description of her as 'a melon, a pineapple, an olive tree, an emerald, and a fox in the snow'. Such powerful sentiments recall Roberta's description of the overwhelming impact of kd's face and voice. Significantly, although both Orlando and Roberta are intrigued by the gender ambiguity of their object of desire, ultimately their desire rests on feminine signifiers such as Sasha's eyes (which looked as if they had been fished from the sea, and therefore could not belong to a boy) and kd's 'beautiful voice', which assured Roberta that her idol was female after all.

In Woolf's novel a desirability associated with gender ambiguity is articulated within a narrative which is, at times, explicitly lesbian. This extract, describing how female Orlando dresses as a man to court a female prostitute, highlights the masculinity of the female Orlando, who, clearly, has lesbian desires:

> The young woman raised her head. It was of the most exquisite shapeliness. The young woman raised her eyes. Orlando saw them to be of a lustre such as is sometimes seen on teapots but rarely in a human face. Through this silver glaze the young woman looked up at him (for a man he was to her) appealing, trembling, fearing. ... To feel her hanging lightly yet like a suppliant on her arm roused in Orlando all the feelings which became a man. She looked, she felt, she talked like one. Yet, having been so lately a woman herself, she suspected that the girl's timidity and her hesitating answers and the very fumbling with the key in the latch and the fold of her cloak and the droop of her wrist were all put on to gratify her masculinity.[37]

The desire for lesbian masculinity is thus clearly apparent in Woolf's novel (which is, in part, a satirical comment on traditional romantic literature, and indeed satirizes *Jane Eyre* quite explicitly at times). Whilst masculine signifiers are important in terms of lesbian identification and recognition, desire may be structured through both masculinity and femininity; I would like to suggest that in the lesbian star/fan context femininity operates to secure the desire *as lesbian*, as *between women*.

Significantly, in the film version of *Orlando*,[38] however, the scene with the prostitute is edited out of the narrative, as are all the points at which desire between the female characters is articulated. Thus, a lesbian audience has frustratingly to negotiate the absence of a lesbian narrative in a film of a book with a lesbian theme. Nevertheless, as Orlando is played by female actor, Tilda Swinton, a lesbian reading becomes possible at the points in the narrative where, in the novel, one would be impossible. Thus the meeting with Sasha becomes a space, not for a reading of male homosexual desire, but, rather, lesbian desire, and a lesbian audience is thus able to identify with this scene in a number of ways.

In this scene, Sasha and (male) Orlando are depicted sitting in a carriage; they kiss passionately, but are disturbed by a passer-by (the threat of discovery is quite common in lesbian romantic exchanges). After the kiss Orlando says *he* is sad (or *she* to the lesbian audience, who, I have discovered through discussions with lesbian friends, insist on reading the character Orlando *as* Tilda Swinton). Sasha then replies, 'But we are together', to which Orlando retorts, 'Yes, now, but what about tomorrow and the day after?' Significantly, the dilemma of impermanence in a moment of passion is more integral to a lesbian romantic encounter than a heterosexual one. Lesbians are much more likely to wonder about the future of their love, because it is socially forbidden and under constant regulation by a heterosexual social order.

Lesbian recognition in the film *Orlando* depends on a lesbian audience *knowing* that Tilda Swinton is a woman. Gender confusion in the idolization of kd lang by her fans is *resolved* by the fan's delight at realizing her female identity. So, although gender misrecognition or drag is often discussed as challenging to a dominant heterosexual order, identifying as a lesbian, recognizing or desiring other lesbians *always* involves having this gender misrecognition resolved in some way. Although masculine signifiers are exalted by the lesbian fans of kd and Martina, it seems that it is a female masculinity specific to lesbian identity, culture and experience that is articulated here.

In an article entitled 'Masculinity as Spectacle'[39] Steve Neale extends Mulvey's argument about the male gaze, although in a different direction. Where Mulvey suggests that in the cinema men look and women are to be looked at, and that women only achieve a position of active spectatorship through a process of masculinization, Neale examines how heterosexual masculinity may be understood as the object of the gaze, as spectacle. He points out that heterosexual masculinity has rarely been examined as such, and suggests ways in which it may be consumed by spectators in the cinema through practices of looking based on narcissistic identification, voyeurism and fetishism.

But how may we apply Neale's argument to the representation of the lesbian idols kd and Martina, and to the readings of these stars by their lesbian fans? I want to suggest that lesbian viewers utilize the feminine spectatorship practices and strategies pinpointed by Stacey[40] to idolize kd and Martina through codes of masculinity. The relationship between kd and Martina and their fans is not one of simple identification, but is specifically informed by sexual desire.

Neale refers to Paul Willemen's article 'Anthony Mann: Looking at the Male',[41] in which Willemen suggests that the unattainability of the male hero for the male spectator is erotic, yet contradictory. Willemen refers to masculinity as spectacle through the psychoanalytic discourse of repressed homosexual narcissism, and thus focuses specifically on a male spectator: '"The viewer's experience is predicated on the pleasure of seeing the male 'exist' (that is walk, move, ride, fight) in or through cityscapes, landscapes or, more abstractly, history."'[42] The following quotes from fans of Martina show how the objectification of masculinity, which refers to how stars move, walk and 'exist', may structure a subject/object relation between women, thus we can see how these lesbian stars *embody* masculinity:

> I have seen her so often on TV over the years (I am 29 now) that I can conjure her up in my head any time I want to think about her walking across the tennis court or striking a winning shot at a weedy opponent.
>
> *(Sadie)*

> I watched every match that was televised that had her in it, even to the point of having a portable TV *and* a radio going at the same time in my office. ... Every time I saw her on court I admired her more and more – her grace, speed, athleticism, talent. She played awesome tennis, and I considered her more attractive each time.
>
> *(Lisa)*

If *sexual desire* structures the methods of *identification* achieved through lesbian fans' reading practices, then this disrupts Mulvey's idea that a woman must read images of woman through a form of heterosexual masculinization. Heterosexual masculinization, in the sense feminist film theorists working within the perimeters of psychoanalytic theory have meant it, does not adequately describe what is happening in this particular lesbian star/fan relationship. Heterosexual masculinization refers to a woman reading 'in the position of a man', because, according to Mulvey,[43] this is the only possible viewing position offered by Hollywood film texts.

Richard Dyer has noted that the ways in which men are represented in male pin-up photography produces instabilities around masculinity.

He suggests that male pin-ups do not 'work' very well for female consumers because, in the act of being looked at, the male model (within the binaries of male/active, female/passive that structure looking relations) tries to deny the reader's look with his tight-lipped benign stare:

> What is at stake is not just male and female sexuality but male and female power. The maintenance of power underpins further instabilities in the image of men as sexual spectacle, in terms of the active/passive nexus of looking, the emphasis on muscularity and the symbolic association of male power and the phallus.[44]

Thus we must question how the instabilities highlighted by Dyer, and the threat to male power that being looked at exerts on the male pin-up model, is played upon, and taken advantage of, in the representation of kd and Martina. For example, in the photograph of Martina that I described in Chapters Three and Four, in which she looks at the camera and bares her flexed muscular arm and clenched fist to the audience, Martina assumes, or is placed in a pose that seems to ironically appropriate male pin-up photography. Her tight-lipped stare may be read as parody of the stare of the male pin-up, and the way she displays her famous lesbian arm muscles could well be interpreted as an ironic reappropriation of the articulations of the masculine male spectacle in the male pin-up photography of both heterosexual and gay culture. Thus, the masculine lesbian pin-up disrupts these different stylistic representations of the male as spectacle which, in their own ways, have enhanced men in dominant positions within a patriarchal society.

Masculine Identifications

Some lesbian fans used the desire for masculinity in their idols in order specifically to point out similarities between their idols and themselves. These narratives of the masculine self demonstrate how masculinity and identification operate in the fans' accounts, and so produce a desire for masculinity. Mistaking kd lang for a man also led some fans to identify with her for that very reason:

> I began seeing kd on MTV. Wondering who the hell this bloke was I recalled that in amongst some of my magazines there had been a couple of interviews advertised. It was much to my amazement that I discovered that HE was in fact a SHE! Let me add something here.

I'm quite tall, I've been taller than most since I was 16. So being 6ft tall and preferring to have short hair and always being keen to follow the popular fashions of student-hood, I wore my Dr Marten boots and jeans, trousers, men's shirts. ... Anyway, I have, since I was 16, had a tendency to be mistaken for a man. Initially it was quite funny, sometimes quite annoying, but now it is hardly an uncommon experience. But, here I was doing exactly what all these people were doing to me – mistaking someone for a man. To say I was intrigued is an understatement.

(Zoe)

In another letter, Miranda pointed out how Martina's masculinity had been important to her own self-image and masculine identification, through a repudiation of conventional femininity:

I just thought she was a beautiful woman. She seemed very strong, slightly more muscular than the fashion was for women. This was 1982, then the media was full of pictures of Princess Diana, who was then very 'frilly', romantic, silly, pretty, plump and blonde. I never liked Princess Di, as all my classmates did, because she was portrayed as lovably stupid. At this point in my life I was trying to get away from this label myself. ... My body got unwanted attention from nearly every man who saw me, it seemed. So I had something of a Princess Di complex. I wanted to get away from this female stereotype, which was beginning to seem like my inevitably doomed fate. Anyway it was hugely refreshing, as you can imagine, to see a totally different type of woman. Her tennis dresses were a bit 'fluffy' but her butchness shone through. I wanted to be like her, or even become her, but it seemed impossible for me to 'unprettify' myself, so I admired her instead.

Personal histories were also important to an identification with masculinity for some of the respondents. This sometimes extended to childhood memories, as this extract about kd from June's letter illustrates: 'She played sport when she was young and rode round town playing at Starsky and Hutch (if the biography is to be believed) which are all the things I did.'

Lesbian fans of kd and Martina desire their idols through intersecting codes of masculinity and femininity, and read in the position of a lesbian, through a lesbian gaze. Looking practices in the lesbian star/fan relationship, then, reproduce the possibility of lesbian desire and identification in a way which confuses the heterosexualized theories of the gaze that have dominated film theory for some years, and which are now beginning to be challenged by feminist theorists such as Stacey.[45]

kd and Country

The idolization of kd by her lesbian fans draws on another masculine discourse: country and western music and dress codes. Country and western has become increasingly popular for lesbians in Britain. This popularity has taken the form of country and western club nights, women-only line dancing and the incorporation of country and western dress codes in lesbian fashion – and, of course, a taste in country music. Although I did not specifically ask respondents to comment on country and western, some did so, and, significantly, through recourse to kd lang's relationship to masculinity.

The appropriation of country and western is often new for kd fans; however, I also received letters from ardent country fans. Lisa wrote about her experience of kd's music:

> I used to like her a lot. I'm a country music fan from way back – long before it became the fashionable thing for a dyke, which I date the origins of to *Desert Hearts* – witness the number of lesbians who name Patsy Cline as one of their favourites, then listen to the soundtrack of that movie!! So I used to like her music – especially the *Shadowlands* album, which I still think of as her best. I liked the way she looked back then – kind of cute. Then she got taken up by the media, came out and went stupid. I hate the hairstyle I've seen her with recently – growing long and falling all over her face – I hate the clothes she's taken to wearing …

Thus, kd and Martina are idolized through many different discourses of masculinity, from the country music genre to the spectacle of the muscular body. The appropriation of country and western music and fashion by lesbians, through the consumption of kd as a spectacle of masculinity, disrupts heterosexuality. This is because, in this lesbian star/fan context, identification and desire combine to disturb the heterosexual premise on which a deeply patriarchal country and western culture turns.

In the lesbian star/fan relationship more generally, it is important to remember that these idols are also desired for their *feminine* attributes – kd's beautiful voice and Martina's blondeness – marking this context of star/fan exchange as specifically lesbian (as I have already argued, their femininity provides a resolution to gender misrecognition). Thus, masculinity and femininity interconnect here in complicated ways which demarcate the characteristics of the lesbian star/fan relationship. Romantic narratives and the lesbian gaze interact through the redeployment of particular meanings of masculinity and femininity within the expression of lesbian culture. However, it is important now to question how this re-signification of gender in this context of lesbian fandom draws on racial discourse.

Lesbian Fandom and Ethnic Identity

The ethnic 'otherness' of kd and Martina was often cited by their fans as a feature which made these stars more attractive. These next two quotes illustrate how the discourse of ethnicity is woven into the narrative of the letters. First, Tiffany partializes kd's body in order to identify elements that she believes reveal her 'Sioux' ancestry:

> I have pictures of kd all over my bedroom wall. I especially collect pictures of her face. She has beautiful features: jet black hair, blue eyes fringed with dark eyelashes, straight nose, high cheekbones. She has incredibly noble features and wonderful bone structure. You can really see the Sioux in her. Her mouth is quite small but voluptuous nonetheless ...

Tiffany's comment about kd's 'Siouxness' draws on the western discourse of racial identity which essentializes particular characteristics within the body of a person: specific features – her blue eyes, her jet black hair and her bone structure – are taken to signify the ethnic otherness which makes kd extra-attractive.

In this next quote, Margot finds Martina more attractive because of her Czechoslovakian national identity:

> I didn't particularly notice Martina until she became famous, and then reading her autobiography made me notice what an open, honest, caring person she was and has always remained. Her Central European

background gives her extra depth, and her striving to reach the very top was admirable.

Here, characteristics such as honesty and openness are identified as belonging to a Czechoslovakian national identity, or as Margot puts it, a 'Central European background'. In contrast to the *bodily* characteristics picked out by Tiffany to signify a Sioux identity, Margot has chosen *personality* traits to define the particularity of Martina's Czech identity. Thus, in western discourses of race, ethnicity and nationalism, a Native American identity apparently resides in the body of a person (as a 'racial' identity), whereas an Eastern European identity seems to inhabit the personality of a person (as a 'national' identity).

Significantly, however, in both cases these 'other' identities are commented upon within the context of a globally dominant western Anglo-American culture, in which a dominant whiteness is repeatedly made invisible by strategies which make visible racially, ethnically or nationally 'other' identities. Thus, it seems that the lesbian star/fan relationship which has opened up greater possibilities for living as lesbians and increased visibility, actually reinforces the strategies of racism and nationalism that pervade western society and reproduce white privilege.

Further, apart from making invisible the strategies of racial and national domination, some fans have exalted and eroticized attributes in Martina which pertain to whiteness as an ideal. In this next quote, Margot has eroticized Martina's blonde hair: 'With her blonde hair she reminds me of sunshine, and it is good to think of such a fine human being in this world which seems to be going to the bad in so many ways.' In another extract, Lisa similarly eroticizes Martina's blonde hair, but also idealizes blonde hair more generally:

> I started buying the odd tennis magazine. Then in a copy of *Tennis Today* in 1981 I spotted an advert for Yonex® racquets, which showed a half page of Billie Jean King and a half page of Martina getting ready for a backhand (I thought that was good, Yonex® the dyke's favourite racquet!!) ... and I thought she's attractive, she's actually quite attractive. Then she went blonde! I've always had a weak spot for blondes (especially with blue or grey eyes) and I was sunk.

Indeed, the way Martina's blonde hair is compared with sunshine or evokes a blonde goddess image in these extracts is reminiscent of the way in which Marilyn Monroe was described by both her fans and the media. In *Heavenly Bodies* Richard Dyer examines the image of the 'blonde goddess' in relation to the stardom of Marilyn Monroe, illustrating how her image reproduces whiteness as ideal: 'Blondeness, especially platinum blondeness, is the ultimate sign of whiteness.'[46] In his article 'White' he has also discussed this idea in relation to the lighting codes of Hollywood cinema, again with particular reference to Monroe:

> the codes of glamour lighting in Hollywood were developed in relation to white women, to endow them with a glow and radiance that has correspondences with the transcendental rhetoric of popular Christianity. Of no woman was this more true than Marilyn Monroe, known by the press at the time as 'the Body' ... her image is an inescapably and necessarily white one; in many of her films this combines with the conventions of glamour lighting to make her disappear as flesh and blood even more thoroughly than is the case with other women stars.[47]

However, the idealization of whiteness in relation to Martina is contradictory because of her gender identity as a masculine lesbian. Dyer argues that blondeness is very specifically not only a signifier of whiteness but also of extreme womanliness: 'in the elaboration of light and dark imagery, the blonde woman comes to represent not only the most desired of woman but also the most womanly of women'.[48] Thus in relation to the representation and idolization of Martina as a masculine blonde lesbian goddess, codes of gender and race interconnect in a highly contradictory manner, disturbing the logic of the western heterosexual discourses of both gender and race. This is not to argue, however, that racial privilege is being challenged by the star/fan relationship here (as I believe heterosexual gender relations are); it is merely to suggest that such a lesbian star/fan context highlights the way racial and gender hierarchies usually work co-operatively in western culture.

Conclusion

In this chapter I have argued that the phenomenon of lesbian fandom challenges heterosexuality in fan cultures. Lesbian fandom achieves a sustained reproduction of lesbian identity, and lesbian fan narratives are radically linked to experiences of coming out. These fan narratives also disrupt the representation of heterosexuality by rewriting romantic discourse through a specifically lesbian desire.

This rewriting of romance takes place in several different ways. First, the special connection the lesbian fan feels for the star underlines how being a lesbian sets one apart from heterosexuality and forms a 'special' part in a person's life; further, this specialness also relates to the public reproduction of kd's and Martina's lesbian identifications, which sanctions lesbian identity in a cultural space. Second, the excessive romantic language in lesbian fan letters brings an intense representation of lesbian desire to the notion of romance, and underscores what is at stake in terms of living and identifying as a lesbian in a deeply homophobic society. Third, lesbian romantic fantasies show that traditional heterosexual romantic strategies may be rearticulated by lesbians, who ransack the heterosexual romantic structure to produce specifically lesbian fantasies and dreams. Fourth, the unattainability of the star, and of the love-object in romantic discourse, translates, in a lesbian context, to the notion of the preciousness and sacredness of a hard-won lesbian identity and culture.

Importantly, in the lesbian star/fan context the lesbian gaze undercuts the heterosexual romantic scenario because a masculine woman is the object of this lesbian gaze, thus disrupting the sex-to-gender causality which marks the heterosexual romantic narrative. Even though this gender misrecognition has to be resolved by the lesbian viewer in order to secure a lesbian exchange, the possibility of gender misrecognition is a pervasive feature of both lesbian desire and lesbian identification, and dislodges the heterosexual logic of recognition of the other.

The romantic traces that I have outlined in this chapter in relation to lesbian fan narratives are underscored by the lesbian vision of the masculine woman and the way in which the lesbian gaze operates in the lesbian star/fan relationship, and in the way lesbians look at lesbians more generally. In the film *Salmonberries* a specifically lesbian gaze sets up a romantic relationship between two women, involving both the sexual desirability of the masculine Kotzebue (kd lang) by the feminine Roswitha (Rosel Zech) and the spectre of gender misrecognition:

> Roswitha refers to (Kotzebue) as a young man. This is of central significance because it appears to reference the common experience of gender confusion among 'butch' or 'visible' lesbians. Several camera angles are used to film this 'moment' of gender confusion. This moment

and their 'look' is also accompanied by periodic flashes of light seeming to come from inside the building. The room is illuminated several times which serves to emphasize the gender mistake by clarifying, through light and visibility, the 'look' operating between the two characters ... Roswitha was *wrong* about Kotzebue's gender and the light flashing on and off seems to invite Roswitha to *see* the *truth*. Consequently, the mistake becomes articulated as a form of challenge – a challenge to Kotzebue to 'show' her 'true' gender; subsequently Kotzebue takes up this challenge by stripping naked in the library and proving her identity.[49]

So, by assessing the ways in which masculine identifications are secured in the lesbian star/fan context, I have suggested that masculinity structures the lesbian romantic narratives of the letters in my study. However, I have also argued that ethnic, national and racial privileges are maintained in this context. This is in line with the traditional representation of white Hollywood stars: as I argued in relation to Dyer's argument,[50] Marilyn Monroe's blonde goddess status is similar to the way in which Martina is idolized. The romantic and objectifying 'othering' of both Martina and kd in terms of race and nationality, by their lesbian fans, operates to keep whiteness as an invisibly dominant category within lesbian culture.

I also suggested that the traditional heterosexual same/other binary, through which heterosexual identities are reproduced, is radically disturbed by the phenomenon of gender misrecognition in lesbian culture. However, the necessary resolution of this gender misrecognition by lesbians has a more sinister side: the daily public gender misrecognition that is part of the lives of many masculine lesbians is resolved by heterosexual culture via an othering of the masculine lesbian as deviant and degenerate. Therefore, however radical the lesbian romantic narrative may be, the regulatory power of heterosexuality consistently resolves the problem that the masculine lesbian poses to heterosexual identity structures. In discussions about lesbian identity which may follow on from my analysis defining the dynamics of this tension must be a central issue.

Notes

1. Lawrence Grossberg, 'Is There a Fan in the House?: The Affective Sensibility of Fandom' in Lisa A. Lewis (ed.), *The Adoring Audience: Fan Culture and Popular Media* (London and New York: Routledge, 1992), pp. 50–65.
2. Henry Jenkins, *Textual Poachers: Television Fans and Participatory Culture* (London: Routledge, 1992), p. 283.
3. John Fiske, 'The Cultural Economy of Fandom' in Lewis (ed.), *The Adoring Audience*, pp. 30–49.
4. This suggestion can also be critiqued on the grounds of racial reductionism, because black male sporting fandom is an important part of black male straight, and gay, cultures, both in the USA and in Britain.
5. Fiske, 'The Cultural Economy of Fandom', p. 33.
6. *Ibid.*, p. 35.
7. Quoted in Fred Vermorel and Judy Vermorel, 'A Glimpse at the Fan Factory' in Lewis (ed.), *The Adoring Audience*, p. 201.
8. *Ibid.*
9. Colin Campbell, *The Romantic Ethic and the Spirit of Modern Consumerism* (London: David Blackwell, 1987).
10. Jackie Stacey, *Star Gazing* (London: Routledge, 1994), p. 140.
11. *Ibid.* p. 141.
12. *Ibid.*, pp. 141–2.
13. *Ibid.*, p. 142.
14. Lynne Pearce and Jackie Stacey (eds), *Romance Revisited* (London: Lawrence and Wishart, 1995), p. 14.
15. For a comprehensive analysis of Harlequin romances and their readers, in relation to feminism, see Janice Radway, *Reading the Romance: Women, Patriarchy and Popular Literature* (Chapel Hill and London: University of North Carolina Press, 1985).
16. Pearce and Stacey, *Romance Revisited*, p. 12.
17. *Ibid.*, p. 15.
18. *Ibid.*, p. 18.
19. Charlotte Brontë, *Jane Eyre* (London: Penguin, 1985, first published in 1847). *Jane Eyre* is a romantic novel that draws on the concerns of the Romantic movement, but also on other literary developments, such as the Gothic novel.
20. *Ibid.*, p. 145.
21. A feature of the mass-market romance, as one would expect, is that they all work to the same format; therefore, my examples are completely random. See Radway, *Reading the Romance*, on Harlequin romances.
22. Helen Bianchin, *The Stefanos Marriage* (Richmond: Mills and Boon, 1991), p. 6.
23. Carol Mortimer, *One Chance at Love* (Richmond: Mills and Boon, 1989), p. 20.
24. Laura Mulvey, 'Visual Pleasure and Narrative Cinema', *Screen*, Vol. 16 No. 3, Autumn 1975, pp. 6–18.
25. Laura Mulvey, 'Afterthoughts on "Visual Pleasure and Narrative Cinema" Inspired by *Duel in the Sun* (King Vidor, 1946)', *Framework: A Film Journal*, 15/16/17, Summer 1981, pp. 12–15.
26. Lorraine Gamman and Margaret Marshment, 'Introduction' in Lorraine Gamman and Margaret Marshment (eds), *The Female Gaze* (London: The Women's Press, 1988), pp. 1–7.
27. *Desperately Seeking Susan*, directed by Susan Seidelman, 1985.

28 *All About Eve*, directed by Joseph L. Mankiewicz, 1950.

29. Jackie Stacey, 'Desperately Seeking Difference' in Gamman and Marshment (eds), *The Female Gaze* Lorraine Gamman and Margaret Marshment (eds), pp. 112–29.

30. Stacey, *Star Gazing*, p. 29.

31. Caroline Evans and Lorraine Gamman discuss the lesbian gaze in 'The Gaze Revisited, or Reviewing Queer Viewing' in Paul Burston and Colin Richardson (eds), *A Queer Romance: Lesbians, Gay Men and Popular Culture* (London and New York: Routledge, 1995), pp. 13–56; however, their theory is premised on the 'queer' idea of the polymorphously perverse that I discussed via Dollimore's theory in Chapter Two. Evans and Gamman suggest that to talk of a 'lesbian gaze' is essentialist. However, the contextualized economy of 'looking relations' could be regarded as one of the ideas that is most *unassimilable* within the notion of essentialism.

32. Stacey, 'Desperately Seeking Difference'.

33. See Christopher Frayling, *Spaghetti Westerns: Cowboys and Europeans from Karl May to Sergio Leone* (London and New York: Routledge, 1981).

34. See Frayling, *ibid.*, for a discussion of the westerns of Sergio Leone, Sergio Corbucci, and others.

35. Virginia Woolf, *Orlando* (London: Vintage Books, 1992, first published in 1928).

36. *Ibid.*, pp 18–19.

37. *Ibid.*, p. 139.

38. *Orlando*, directed by Sally Potter, 1992.

39. Steve Neale, 'Masculinity as Spectacle', *Screen*, Vol. 24 No. 6, November–December 1983, pp. 2–16.

40. Stacey, *Star Gazing*.

41. Paul Willemen, 'Anthony Mann: Looking at the Male', *Framework: A Film Journal*, 15/16/17, Summer 1981, pp. 16–20.

42. Willemen, 'Anthony Mann', quoted in Steve Neale, 'Masculinity as Spectacle', p. 8.

43. Mulvey, 'Visual Pleasure and Narrative Cinema'.

44. Richard Dyer, 'Don't Look Now: The Instabilities of the Male Pin-up', *Screen*, Vol. 23 Nos 3–4, 1982, pp. 61–71.

45. Stacey, *Star Gazing*.

46. Richard Dyer, *Heavenly Bodies: Film Stars and Society* (London: BFI/Macmillan, 1992), p. 43.

47. Richard Dyer, 'White', *Screen*, Vol. 29 No. 4, Autumn 1988, p. 63.

48. Dyer, *Heavenly Bodies*, p. 45.

49. Louise Allen, 'Salmonberries: Consuming kd lang', in Tamsin Wilton (ed.), *Immortal Invisible: Lesbians and the Moving Image* (London and New York: Routledge,1995), p. 71.

50. Dyer, *Heavenly Bodies*.

6

Craving the Constant

Martina's tennis career, her gender positioning in opposition to feminine Chris Evert, her engagement in political activism and stories about her love life have been consistently reproduced through a visual narrativization of lesbianism for almost twenty years. kd's music career, her visual representation on album covers, television and video have followed a similar path. Such visual narrativization of lesbianism as a lived identity has enabled the reproduction of lesbian culture over two decades of visual media. However, it has also been accompanied by the representation of the lesbian chic image in mainstream media. This unprecedented coverage of lesbians in the media would have been unheard of fifteen, or even ten, years ago. Thus, in this book I have concentrated on the distinctive and contemporary importance of such proliferate representation of lesbianism in the dominant media, and the reception of these images by lesbian consumers.

On the one hand, then, I have argued that the representation of a specifically feminine lesbian identity in the mainstream media, embodied in lesbian chic, is a reactionary move on the part of heterosexual culture in the 1990s, as it reproduces lesbianism as an impermanent, unstable and superficial category.[1] However, on the other hand, I have also pointed out how the importance of kd and Martina for lesbian fans signifies that lesbians produce innovative, generative and transformative strategies in order to counteract dominant heterosexual ideology.

I have argued that the way gender privilege operates in relation to the representation of lesbianism in Britain in the 1990s inscribes the masculine lesbian as deviant and abnormal; by contrast, the feminine lesbian is presented to heterosexual culture in the palatable form of lesbian chic. However, a crucial point in relation to this gender-privileging system is that lesbian chic undermines what it means to identify as either a masculine *or* a feminine lesbian. In my view *living out* a feminine lesbian identity is equally unpalatable to heterosexuals, because living as a feminine *or* masculine lesbian undercuts the supposed superficiality of the lesbian identity that is implied in the mainstream representation of lesbian chic.

I would argue that heterosexuals are equally threatened and disturbed by both masculine and feminine lesbians, but in markedly different ways. Further study in the area of lesbian identity should concentrate on the significant differences between the lesbian femme and both the heterosexual woman and the lesbian chic image, examining the visual and other signifiers that operate to constitute the femme as a lesbian both within lesbian and straight cultural spaces. Thus I have not attempted to argue that masculine lesbians are more deconstructive of heterosexuality than feminine lesbians, because in the end I am not interested in the question of whether different lesbian identities are politically correct or not. What I have maintained, though, is that when a specifically lesbian gender difference is represented in the mainstream media (the difference between the masculine and feminine lesbian identity), a sense of lesbian identity and culture is *displaced* through the ways in which femininity is deployed in order to ground the lesbian chic figure in a dominant heterosexual regime of sex and gender meanings. The mainstream representation of lesbian chic places fashion, make-up and other signifiers of femininity at the centre of what it means to be a lesbian, rather than 'ways of living'.[2]

Sarah Schulman's assertion[3] that images produced by both the mainstream and the lesbian and gay media are at times indistinguishable is a worrying thought, particularly when one considers how lesbian masculinity is portrayed as abhorrent and when even the lesbian-oriented media often attempts to reproduce a feminized lesbian identity as ideal. Even though certain lesbian and mainstream cultural productions may challenge heterosexuality through the deployment of parody or appropriation (for example, *Desert Hearts*, as Stacey argued,[4] and the British television series *You Rang M'Lord*[5]), representation of a feminized lesbian identity in soaps and films is misrepresentative of lesbian culture and identity and unproblematically reproduces a heterosexualized sex-to-gender causality whereby lesbianism becomes 'acceptable' if it has a feminine face.[6]

One attempt to counter a heterosexist demonization of lesbianism and homosexuality has been through a celebration of lesbian and gay deviance and perversity in some recent films, either directed by lesbians or gays, and labelled 'queer cinema' (for example, Tom Kalin's *Swoon*, 1991), or received by lesbian or gay audiences as 'queer cinema'[7] (for example, Michael Winterbottom's *Butterfly Kiss*, 1995). In rejecting the notion that lesbians and gays must present themselves as acceptable to heterosexual culture, queer cinema may be argued to depict lesbians and gays as a dangerous threat to heterosexual culture. However, we must ask how lesbians and gays are engaging with such films in the cinema audience. How far do these films offer possibilities for recognition and identification in the viewing context?

In my view, queer cinema ultimately only *highlights* heterosexual knowledge systems, but does not *act on* or *apart from* heterosexuality. This is because queer cinema does not reproduce a sense of lesbian identity, facilitate lesbian identifications, or offer possibilities for the reproduction of lesbian culture, as the readings possible in relation to queer films consistently draw the lesbian or gay viewer into a resistive dialogue with the regulative power of heterosexuality.

Furthermore, the trends in recent academic thought which interlock poststructuralist theory with queer (as exemplified in the writings of Dollimore and Sedgwick) coincide with this notion of lesbian identity as impermanent and superficial. Judith Butler's now famous study of identity in her various books and articles, Eve Sedgwick's analyses, and many more articles by lesbian theorists have been consumed and regurgitated as one word – *performativity*. In relation to this word, meanings around shifting identities and impermanent structures of living have been sanctified as new and innovative ways of being and theorizing; in contrast, ways of thinking about the development of cultures and modes of identification have been sacrificed. In other words in recent theories of identity, and in 'lifestyle' politics, the slipperiness of identity and meanings are understood to explain all forms of cultural and social exchange, while ways of thinking about lesbian identity and culture as stable and coherent have been lost.

It has been important to examine the route that queer has taken in the academy because notions of queer and performativity have become so pervasive in relation to theoretical (and not so theoretical) studies of lesbianism, lesbian identity and lesbian culture. Queer theory is thus not unrelated to the representation of lesbian chic in the mainstream media, in that whilst queer theory is deployed in lesbian theory, it also invisibilizes lesbian identity. I believe that Butler is a lesbian theorist, and not a queer theorist, as the centrality of lesbianism and lesbian identity and the resistance to heterosexual hegemony characterizes her work. Further, her understanding of performativity is determined by an understanding of power relations. I would argue that Dollimore and Sedgwick are queer theorists *because* their theories exclude the possibility of the analysis of lesbianism. The distinction is crucial.

Another most striking issue in relation to these two faces of lesbian representation I have examined – lesbian chic and lesbian idols – is that of *identification*. The accounts of lesbian fans reveal how their identification with their idols facilitates a reproduction and proliferation of lesbian culture which challenges heterosexualized meanings of sex and gender. It seems plausible that the vision of the masculine woman signifies lesbianism to both lesbian and straight audiences alike, engendering horror and fear in heterosexual audiences of popular culture. This phenomenon highlights the importance of the visual in contemporary western culture.

Characters in soaps, such as Beth in *Brookside* and Zoe in *Emmerdale*, and middle-class women experimenting with lesbian sex in the pages of *Harpers and Queen*[8] are represented as lesbians via spoken dialogue or the written word. However, it seems clear to me that, because lesbian identification is occurring between kd and Martina and their fans in terms of the visual (the masculine woman as a sign of lesbianism), this means that lesbian identity is communicable through a kind of *visual narrativity*. This visual narrativity is of crucial importance to lesbian identifications and culture as it produces a visual dialogic space which cuts across regulatory regimes of power. In other words, the proliferation of visual iconography in late twentieth-century western society facilitates strategies of visual identification which *escape* the regulatory regime of heterosexuality.

Nevertheless, as I have illustrated, these strategies are always under threat of recuperation by, for example, the representation of lesbian chic. Thus, in the 1990s, the importance of the masculine woman as a visual signifier of lesbianism has been undermined by the heterosexist appropria-tion of the feminine lesbian and the mainstream media's rejection of 'old style' masculine lesbian identities as abject beings. That the horrific presence of masculine lesbians persists in the heterosexual imagination is evidenced by this hyper-feminizing and heterosexualizing strategy.

The message, in a 'swinging' 1990s culture of queer identity and lesbian chic, is that masculine lesbians are decidedly out of date. Thus, representations of queer and chic undercut perhaps the most pervasive and consistent route to identifying as a lesbian. Therefore, instead of proliferating opportunities for lesbian identifications (as the representation of lesbians in soaps may at first suggest), in an increasingly reactionary heterosexual culture, possibilities for lesbian recognition are closing down. Significantly, this space of lesbian recognition, offered by the sign of the masculine woman, is not only a space within which masculine lesbians can recognize each other, it is also a place where feminine lesbians may recognize the signs of lesbian culture. This site of recognition is so central to lesbian culture that all forms of lesbian identity are being threatened by the heterosexist underpinnings of the lesbian chic image.

Throughout this book I have argued that the (re)construction of meaning that takes place in lesbian culture, and through lesbian identifications, does so in an ineluctable relation to the visual. This relationship demands that we think about lesbian ways of looking, or gazing, that are specific to lesbian culture and lesbian identificatory strategies. My discussion of the lesbian gaze in this book argued not for a fixed looking position irrespective of subjective experience as a lesbian, nor for a singular meaning produced by lesbian audiences, but for an examination of the ways in which transformative meanings are produced through lesbian looking practices. Being a lesbian necessarily involves the issue of looking or not looking like a lesbian – lesbian looking relations therefore depend on the visual signifiers of lesbian identity whereby lesbians can recognize themselves and each other. However, I suggested that in the context of the lesbian star/fan relationship, lesbian looking relations should be understood in terms of the reproduction of a white ideal and the racial or ethnic 'other'. Looking like a lesbian always entails partaking of the visual signifiers that demarcate the 'lesbian identity' as white. In *Salmonberries*, for example, lesbian gender meanings are secured at the expense of a Native American identification.[9]

So, what can we conclude about how the categories of gender and sex are re-signified in the context of the lesbian star/fan relationship? How can we understand the categories of masculinity and femininity, and of man and woman, in relation to the analysis of lesbian identification and culture that I have made here? The stardom of kd and Martina as famous masculine lesbians must alter how we think about the notion of 'woman', because these are women who are idealized and idolized for their masculinity. This dynamic changes both the notion of masculinity and the category of woman. One way to show how the meaning of 'woman' shifts in a specifically lesbian context is to look at the idea of gender misrecognition. As I argued in relation to the films *Salmonberries* and *Orlando*, and in relation to fans' accounts, gender misrecognition amongst lesbians must always be resolved in order to secure a lesbian identity, as lesbianism is marked by a desire *between women*. Here, then, the category 'woman' is not a shifting signifier but, importantly, a stable, constant, and authentic signifier of the possibility of lesbianism. The representations of masculine lesbian stars in the media forces a rethinking of the category woman. However, it does not become less stable, or more superficial in this context but, rather, is understood by lesbians in relation to specific understandings of masculinity and femininity which cannot be grafted onto heterosexual knowledge systems. In other words, in a lesbian context the meaning of woman *shifts* but into a place of *alternative coherence* rather than a state of eternal instability; in lesbian culture masculinity and femininity signify in very different ways from how they signify in heterosexual culture. These alternative meanings of masculinity and femininity consequently bear on meanings of man and woman – a lesbian woman is different from a heterosexual woman because of *culture*, and the *cultural meanings* of 'woman' in relation to those two different identities. So, Monique Wittig can and cannot have it her way – lesbians both *are* and *are not* women.[10]

However, the alternative meaning of woman in a lesbian context can have the effect of prioritizing white womanhood as ideal. Indeed, kd and Martina are consumed by their lesbian fans within an arena of looking relations specific to stardom that privileges whiteness as ideal. Throughout this book I have pointed out ways in which whiteness is prioritized in terms of the rearticulation of gender in a lesbian star/fan relationship, and within lesbian culture. Gendered visibility in western culture relies for coherence on white privileging ways of looking and iconography. In a specifically lesbian context of gender rearticulation these processes of white idealization may be highlighted, but this does not mean to say that they are undercut or disturbed.

In my discussion of masculine lesbian identifications, and the appropriative work done by the lesbian pin-up, I have suggested that, although in this lesbian star/fan context desire is often structured through masculinity, and even gender ambiguity, it also is structured through the idea of lesbian authenticity – kd and Martina are desired because they live out authentic, constant and coherent lesbian identities. Authenticity, constancy and coherence sets *lesbian gender* apart from heterosexual knowledge systems. The 'lesbian look', or the 'lesbian gaze', disrupts the heterosexual sex-to-gender causality when this gaze is structured (as I would argue it usually is) by a specifically lesbian masculinity; but this disruption is, importantly, underpinned by the understanding of a consistently lived-out lesbian identity, within an identifiable lesbian culture that has developed over time.

I have analysed the notion of gender in great depth in this book, but what of sex? What of those categories of male and female that are popularly located in relation to sex, as opposed to the gender categories of man and woman? In trying to understand what the notion of sex might mean in relation to lesbianism, my first thought was to examine the difference between sex and gender; but in popular usage in lesbian culture, the terms seem to be interchangeable. However, on further reflection I began to identify contexts within which lesbians are referred to as 'female': in a hospital; in a police station; in a court of law and in a doctor's surgery. Therefore, it seems that, for lesbians, being female is a site of social regulation. Further, sex categories, in terms of how and where lesbians become female, seem to relate to all kinds of heterosexual reproduction – the reproduction of bodies, rights, knowledges, patriarchy and so on.

As I began to question when a lesbian becomes a female, I realized that the answer was 'not very often'. A heterosexual woman is female more often than a lesbian because her identity is constructed in terms of a heterosexuality which turns on an understanding of sex both as a categorical and as an act, which conceptually operate together at the conjuncture of *heterosexualized bodily reproduction*. It therefore occurred to me that a lesbian is a woman in a way which is specific to lesbianism, but that she is a female when the object of heterosexual inspection and regulation.

The concepts of gender and sex become meaningful in relation to the signs of a specific culture. So, it seems that in the context of lesbian experience and lesbian knowledges there is, so to speak, 'no sex for lesbians': lesbians do not have a sex except when being regulated by heterosexual regimes of power. In the lesbian star/fan relationship, the female sex of the idol and the fan strangely disappears because of the unimportance of being female in relation to lesbian identifications and lesbian culture; indeed, it has taken me six chapters to reach the subject of sex in this book. However, in the representation of lesbian chic in the mainstream media, sex is most definitely an issue, because such representations are produced in the context of heterosexual regulation and for heterosexual consumption, where sexual difference is all important.

Consequently, meanings of sex and gender are determined by the different configurations of power across different sites of cultural reproduction.

Thus, a lesbian is a woman in a way that only a lesbian can be, and masculinity and femininity become identificatory strategies whereby the meaning of woman may be understood in lesbian knowledge systems. Here, then, woman has a coherent meaning. Conversely, to talk of lesbians in relation to sex makes little sense in terms of lesbian ways of living: there is no word for 'sex', or rather, *no concept of sexual difference*, in lesbian cultural languages. Further, lesbian sexual practice *only* has a relationship to the regulation of lesbian bodies through a binaristic social order (sexual difference) when lesbians are regulated by heterosexuality in terms of their sexual practices. In other words, 'having sex' is certainly important to lesbians, but not in the way that 'having sex' is important to heterosexuals. In fact, in terms of signifying systems within a specific culture, the two acts are so far apart that it hardly makes sense to talk about them in relation to each other at all. For heterosexuals the sex act cements the fact that gender difference is determined by sexual difference, a concept that is irrelevent for lesbians. Therefore, if heterosexual domination does not 'make sense' to lesbians, then neither does the sexual difference through which lesbian bodies are inscribed as abject in heterosexual knowledge systems. When lesbians engage in lesbian culture and make lesbian identifications they, in effect, 'step out of sex'. Therefore, to argue that gender is 'playful' does not adequately describe what lesbians 'do' with gender – namely, reproduce the coherence of gender, but inscribe it with a specifically lesbian meaning where sexual difference is irrelevent to practice.

What I have been suggesting throughout this book is that lesbian theory should interrogate the relationships between sex, gender and sexuality via an analysis of the identifications and cultural specificities that have developed over time and characterize lesbianism. To achieve action and change from a subordinated position involves continuously re-evaluating the dialogue between lesbian cultural reproduction and the cultural reproduction of the wider dominating society. This is a particularly difficult task when this subordinated space of lesbian cultural reproduction is complicated by the workings of racism and classism. Therefore, studying lesbian culture and modes of lesbian identification necessarily involves analysing further power struggles. The multi-textual analysis I have made here contains possibilities for mapping processes of white idealization and racial and ethnic othering, and these discourses should be traced in a way which provides a critique of the exclusions across and through which all identifications are produced and lived.

Further, if woman signifies differently in a lesbian context; if the meaning of woman has shifted here, in terms of the reappropriative strategies of lesbian gender systems, then does this shifting of the category of woman to an alternative coherence also shift white idealism and privilege into a similar position, whereby the idealism of whiteness is still upheld? One of the ways that I have tried to understand the consumption of representations of lesbianism is through highlighting how racial privileges are often resecured in the lesbian star/fan relationship. However, I have also stressed that this form of analysis highlights the inconsistencies, gaps and contradictions in the rearticulation of whiteness as ideal within a lesbian context. For example, I have stressed how *gendered visibility* structures strategies whereby racial othering often takes place and white idealism is frequently secured. I have suggested that 'parts' of identity such as race, ethnicity, nationality, gender and sex can never be separated out, yet are always in conflict with each other in relation to representational sites and modes of consumption – Martina is desired for her masculinity, but images of her are produced and consumed through the codes of stardom which represent white womanhood as ideal.

So, we must keep on asking questions about identity – how it is produced and how it relates to the development of cultures and cultural specificity. I have concentrated on the lesbian star/fan relationship, but what are the other routes by which lesbians mean 'woman' in relation to lesbian culture and identity? How are we to understand the importance of the masculine woman in lesbian culture in terms of the various feminine lesbian identity positions that also make lesbian culture specific? How can we (as we must) separate the notion of lesbian chic from the feminine lesbian identity? How can we produce analyses of lesbian identity and culture which expose, and work on, racial privileges that secure white lesbian identities as lesbian ideals? How can we understand lesbian meanings of gender, sex and masculinity and femininity in relation to race, nation, ethnicity, religion and class in other ways, apart from in the lesbian star/fan relationship? In this book I have highlighted the need for field studies so that we can map out the cultural reproduction of lesbianism across various textual and social arenas, so that we may begin to take more rigorous approaches to understanding lesbian cultural specificity and the exclusionary forces that operate against it, and *through* it.

A central concern has been to stress the importance of a multi-textual analysis of lesbian identity and culture that interconnects trends in the academy (queer theory and psychoanalysis), in identity politics (lesbian chic and queer), visual iconography relating to lesbianism, and the personal narratives of lesbian consumers. Combining the fans' accounts with detailed examinations of visual materials and theoretical concerns, I have posed specific questions about how meanings of gender are reconstituted through continuous and coherent lesbian *ways of living*. I have also shown that the visual pervasiveness of lesbian 'gender difference' undermines the way gender and sex signify outside a heterosexual regulative knowledge system, through charting recent dominant heterosexist moves to feminize the lesbian image and to increasingly suppress possibilities for lesbian recognition, identity and cultural reproduction.

I have suggested that we see lesbian identificatory strategies and culture as generative, innovative and transformative sites of meaning production that trouble or disrupt dominant heterosexual meanings about sex and gender, but I have also stressed that the feminized representations of lesbian chic are a heterosexist reappropriation and recuperation of lesbian ways of living and being. Modes of identifying as a lesbian and the reproduction of lesbian culture are under continuous threat from reactionary strategies that aim to resecure heterosexual regulation and domination. Hence, future studies into lesbian identity and culture must be developed which fully interrogate identificatory trends and movements in late twentieth-century society and their consequences for how we live our lives as lesbians.

Notes

1. See Laura Cottingham, *Lesbians Are So Chic ... That We're Not Really Lesbians At All* (London and New York: Cassell, 1996).

2. For an analysis of culture in terms of 'ways of living' see Raymond Williams, *Keywords: A Vocabulary of Culture and Society* (London: Fontana Press, 1988).

3. Sarah Schulman, 'Now a Word from Our Sponsor: The Emergence of a Gay Management Class and its Impact on the Print Media', a paper given at the University of California at San Diego, 17 January 1994, pp. 1–15.

4. Donna Deitch's famous lesbian film *Desert Hearts* (1985) is argued to be

a parodic reappropriation and perversion of the traditional heterosexual romantic film in an excellent article by Jackie Stacey: '"If You Don't Play, You Can't Win": *Desert Hearts* and the Lesbian Romance Film' in Tamsin Wilton (ed.), *Immortal, Invisible: Lesbians and the Moving Image* (London and New York: Routledge, 1995), pp. 92–114.

5. The British television comedy *You Rang M'Lord* (BBC 1, 1988–1993) contains a long-term lesbian character Sissy, who, in this camp *Upstairs Downstairs* spoof set in the 1930s, is a butch Radclyffe Hall figure and plays alongside a femme counterpart. The appreciation of this series as parody by lesbian audiences is possible, I would argue, by the way in which the heterosexual characters are comically shocked, and yet also bewilderingly accepting, of Sissy's lesbian antics, which are played upon to produce shock-value satirical comedy scenes. In my view Sissy's central role as a comedic lesbian protagonist produces a reading of this series which destabilizes heterosexual privilege and is instantly appealing for a gay and lesbian audience.

6. Again refer to Cottingham, 'Lesbians Are So Chic', for a detailed discussion of lesbian representation in the mainstream media from this point of view.

7. For a discussion of queer cinema see Bad Object Choices (eds), *How Do I Look? Queer Film and Video* (Seattle: Bay Press, 1991); Martha Gever, John Greyson and Pratibha Parmar (eds), *Queer Looks: Perspectives on Lesbian and Gay Film and Video* (London and New York: Routledge, 1993); B. Ruby Rich, 'New Queer Cinema', *Sight and Sound*, Vol. 2 No. 5, September 1992, pp. 30–5; and for a discussion of queer popular culture see Paul Burston and Colin Richardson, (eds), *A Queer Romance: Lesbians, Gay Men and Popular Culture* (London and New York: Routledge, 1995). A couple of films representative of this movement are *Swoon* (directed by Tom Kalin, 1992) and *Butterfly Kiss* (directed by Michael Winterbottom, 1995).

8. Charlotte Cripps and Laura Tennant, 'Sappho So Good', *Harpers and Queen*, June 1994, pp. 122–7.

9. Louise Allen, 'Salmonberries: Consuming kd lang' in Tamsin Wilton (ed.), *Immortal Invisible: Lesbians and the Moving Image* (London and New York: Routledge, 1995).

10. Monique Wittig, 'The Straight Mind' in *The Straight Mind and Other Essays* (Hemel Hempstead: Harvester Wheatsheaf, 1992), pp. 21–32.

Index